Wychwood

THE SECRET COTSWOLD FOREST

Also by Mollie Harris

A Kind of Magic

Another Kind of Magic

The Green Years

The Archers Country Cookbook

Country Cooking from Pebble Mill

From Acre End

A Drop O' Wine

Cotswold Privies

The Magic of the Cotswold Way

The Cotswold Country Cookbook

Where the Windrush Flows

Privies Galore

Wychwood

THE SECRET
COTSWOLD FOREST

MOLLIE HARRIS

Illustrations GARY WOODLEY

ALAN SUTTON

First published in the United Kingdom in 1991
Alan Sutton Publishing Limited · Phoenix Mill · Far Thrupp · Stroud
Gloucestershire

First published in the United States of America in 1991
Alan Sutton Publishing Inc · Wolfeboro Falls · NH 03896–0848

British Library Cataloguing in Publication Data

Harris, Mollie
Wychwood : the secret Cotswold forest.
1. Oxfordshire (England)
I. Title II. Woodley, Gary
942.571

ISBN 0-86299-788-7

Library of Congress Cataloging in Publication Data
applied for

Typeset in 12/16 Garamond.
Typesetting and origination by
Alan Sutton Publishing Limited.
Colour separation by
Yeo Valley Reproductions.
Printed by
New InterLitho
S.p.A., Milan, Italy.

Contents

ix

ACKNOWLEDGEMENTS

xi

Spring comes to Wychwood

xiii

INTRODUCTION

xvii

DIALECT WORDS AND EXPRESSIONS

xx

MAP OF WYCHWOOD

1

CHAPTER ONE

January

A Winter Walk in Wychwood

11

CHAPTER TWO

February

King Alfred's Cakes

23

CHAPTER THREE

March

Razor Strops and Jew's Ears

33

CHAPTER FOUR

April

Spanish Liquor and Blackthorn Winter

42

CHAPTER FIVE

May

Orchids and Archangels

52

CHAPTER SIX

June

Aspen Trees and Deadly Nightshade

62

CHAPTER SEVEN

July

Blue Fields and Butterflies

71

CHAPTER EIGHT

August

Forest Flowers and Forest Folk

_____

CONTENTS

82

CHAPTER NINE

September

Autumn Crocus and Larch Cones

92

CHAPTER TEN

October

Spiders Webs and Satan's Cherries

100

CHAPTER ELEVEN

November

Sleeping Snails and Squittering Squirrels

110

CHAPTER TWELVE

December

The Last Walk and the Last Words on Wychwood

121

Winter in Wychwood

Acknowledgements

I would especially like to thank Mr and Mrs Bill Archer, Charlie Barnes, Jim Brannan, Mr W.D. (Bill) Campbell, Mr J.M. Campbell, David Dawson, the late Margaret Dermody, Ruth Kench, Peter and Brenda MacGregor, Mr A. Piper, David Rogers, Lord Rotherwick, Mr P. Sheasby, and Mr and Mrs Bill Whittington.

My main sources of information were David Rogers, Chief Warden, Crockham Common Newbury (Nature Conservancy); John Kibble; Woodstock Museum; Beryl Shuman; Sara Wise, and D.H. Alport.

Spring comes to Wychwood

See, dawns breaks, painting leaf and tree
Old Wychwood dons its robe of green.
Now, at our feet, what joy to see
Its rolling sweep of glorious sheen.

Fair scenes, here beast and bird
Find safe retreat 'gainst mans alarm
Rare blossoms too, by lake and sward
Come to perfection, safe from harm.

from John Kibble's book,
Historical and notes on Wychwood, 1928

To lovers of the countryside
and all those who try to
preserve it.

Mollie Harris

Introduction

Wychwood forest lies on the eastern slopes of the Cotswold hills, in an area between the Rivers Windrush and Evenlode. It is the remains of a very extensive royal forest which at one time covered much of the region which is now Oxfordshire. Today Wychwood consists of the largest continuous area of ancient broadleaved forest in Oxfordshire, and centuries ago it was well known for its great oaks. It is said that King Philip of Spain ordered the Spanish Armada to bring back prized oaks from Wychwood and it is believed that Nelson's flagship was built from Wychwood oaks.

Today there are still many fine oaks along with beech, maple and ash, with coppices of hawthorn and hazel, and shrubs of sallow, privet, spindle-berry and blackthorn, with a vast area of newly planted trees of several varieties. Much of the forest is a National Nature Reserve, very rich in flora and containing over 360 species of flowering plants and ferns, many of which are associated with ancient woodland. Over sixty types of mosses and liverwort can be found there as well as eighty-five different sorts of lichen. There are also four 'marl ponds' in the forest that contain several rare water insects and crayfish, as well as aquatic flora. If you are wondering what a 'marl pond' is, it is a pond containing a lot of lime and clay which is a very valuable fertilizer for farmland and most likely very widely used in the old days.

The old name for Wychwood was HWICCE, after a Saxon tribe who settled near there, but there is evidence of folk living there before 3,000 BC. Centuries ago, newcomers from the Continent also settled there: these people knew how to make pottery and use stone, flint and bone for tools; rough buildings were erected for living quarters, and there is evidence that they also built long barrows for their dead. One such 'barrow', 'Barry Hill Tump', can still be seen just outside the village of Leafield on the Charlbury road. It is 350 feet round and 11 feet high, planted with several trees on top and is quite noticeable from the road.

But, as a royal hunting forest, Wychwood was often visited by several kings and queens of England. Edward the Confessor, last of the Saxon kings, who was born at Islip in Oxfordshire, often hunted there. And at Langley, a hamlet near to the

---

village of Leafield which is now just outside the forest boundary, there are a few remains of a hunting lodge. According to the tradition the lodge was once known as Langley Palace, and it was erected by King John. Both King Henry VII and Henry VIII stayed there, together with Henry VIII's daughters. King James also stayed there while on hunting expeditions. An entry in the Parish Register at Shipton-under-Wychwood mentions the death of a French boy who was buried there in September 1603 – 'The court then lying at Langley'. But, after Charles I's time, the place was deserted and in time became a farmhouse, and – as I understand – still is to this day. Later on there was a manor built at Woodstock (which was Crown property at that time), and kings and queens often stayed there when they came to hunt at Wychwood. A similar place was built in Cornbury Park as a shooting lodge – a very different building than that of today. In Queen Elizabeth I's reign, Cornbury Mansion, which is now part of Wychwood, belonged to the Earl of Leicester, and the story goes that one day he was returning there when the ghost of his first wife, Amy Robsart (it was widely believed that he had killed her by pushing her down the stairs at Cumnor Place), appeared before him as he rode up the beautiful avenue known as 'The Broad Light'. She warned him that within ten days he would be with her. Shortly afterwards he fell ill and died – within the time that Amy's ghost had stated. Since then, The Broad Light is supposed to be haunted by Amy Robsart: legend has it that those unfortunate enough to see her will soon die.

Except for one day at Whitsuntide, no-one but the reigning king and his friends could hunt in Wychwood forest. By ancient rights, however, some of the towns and villages along the forest borders could hunt one day a year. The 'Whit Hunt', as it was called, was the most important event in a week of local celebrations, including horn-blowing contests, morris dancing, processions and feasting. The towns and villages were allowed one deer apiece. The head and the antlers and the cut-up skin went to the man or men who were first in at the kill, then the cut-up meat was given to the local inhabitants. Of course, since that time the morris dancing – except for a few breaks inbetween – has survived in a few of the forest villages. Leafield had one morris dance called 'The Leafield nutting dance', and when morris men dance these days at Bampton-in-the-Bush, once part of the medieval forest, they are accompanied by a man who carries a cake in a tin on top of a pole and sometimes in a tin attached to his hat; this is given to the villagers, as a reminder of the time when the meat of the 'Whit' deer was carried on the top of a pole and distributed to the villagers by the morris men.

But the forest laws were very strict and in 1617 some of the surrounding villages petitioned to be free of these laws. They were Old Woodstock, Bladon, Stonesfield, Combe and Hanborough, since, as they pointed out, they were no longer actually in the forest, and although they were successful, King Charles I later tried to extend the forest in 1638 to include those villages again, but he was unsuccessful.

Then in 1853 Wychwood was disafforested and nine years later the Enclosure Act came in to force, which was a sad blow for those folk who lived around the forest, and they lost many of their rights that they had held for centuries. Some of them had got part, or all, of their living from either collecting wood or selling it; then there were furze branches that folk bought to enable them to sweep their chimneys, and birds eggs to help with feeding the families. Nuts were also gathered and sold for the extract of oil as well as for eating. Other folk had common rights and could turn out their cattle in there. Some had herds of swine who, in the autumn, lived in the forest for weeks as there were acorns aplenty, which were guaranteed to put a good few inches of fat on the animals before they were slaughtered for winter food.

A good deal of poaching went on, and one way of catching a deer was to stick a garden fork, wrong way up in the ground, so that the tines were sticking upwards, in a spot where deer usually leapt. The animal would then be impaled on the fork, and great feastings would follow. Gypsies used to dig a big hole and bury the carcass of deer along with hares and rabbits to hide them from the keepers. Then they would cover the hole back over with soil and light a fire on the top and be very innocently sitting around the fire drinking tea when the keepers came round.

Nevertheless, one or two of the ancient rights still remain. I understand that some villages still have the right to enter the forest on a special half day to pick up a 'burden of wood' – Leafield on Tuesdays, Ramsden and Finstock on Thursdays – just what they can carry in their arms, as no wheeled vehicles are allowed in there. The other old custom still kept up today, is visiting the wells on Palm Sunday, or Spanish Liquor Day as many call it. But you can read the full details of this in Chapter Four.

After the Enclosure, thousands of trees were cut down, acres of woodland and heath broken up and several farms were created, many of which still exist today. Now, Wychwood – or 'The Secret Forest' as some people call it – consists of about 1,400 acres of woodlands which also includes Cornbury Mansion and estate. But there are pockets of land and farms in the area which are still Crown property.

In 1989, however, The Ramblers Association, along with many local people, won the right – after fighting for twenty-four years – for the general public to walk through *part* of this wonderful forest. The designated walk is well sign-posted and walkers are asked to keep *strictly to the paths* and not wander away from them. In this way the ancient flora will remain protected and no damage will be done to trees and shrubs, all of which are rare and valuable to the work of scientists to enable future generations to learn about this medieval forest.

Apart from the designated walk, the Wychwood forest remains *strictly private* and I had to acquire, from the owner Lord Rotherwick, special written permission to allow myself and Gary Woodley – the Illustrator – to walk through the Secret Forest during the year 1990, to glean the knowledge to be able to write this book. So, dear reader, come with me and enjoy in words and pictures an imaginary walk through this wonderful Secret Forest, through the seasons of the year, the folklore, poaching stories, light-hearted history and, above all, the wonderful flora and fauna which makes Wychwood forest a very special place.

Horse chestnut

Dialect Words and Expressions

(Many of these were once used in the Wychwood area.)

Arternun	– afternoon
Bwoy	– boy
Cheer	– a chair
Cwut	– coat
Dumel	– slow, dull or stupid
Dee-dee	– secretive
Egg on	– to encourage, to fight, etc.
Holler	– to shout
Howzen	– houses
Hi-nuns	– onions
Lappen	– foolish
Maggled	– hot and tired
Okurd	– awkward
Parkie	– cold
Scrobble	– to scrape up
Shick shac	– oak leaves carried on 29 May
Slans	– sloes
Slummocky	– untidy
Shirty	– cross with someone
Sharlocks	– shallots
A wiffling wind	– changeable
In the burra	– a sheltered place
They be um!	– here they are; or these are they
Lev em bide	– leave them alone
Yer us be!	– here we are
Brevet	– to look for

WYCHWOOD
The Secret Cotswold Forest

Mosen, genral allus	– generally
Pernickety	– fastidious
To and agen	– said of a fickle person
Work-brittle	– fond of work
Clackett	– noise
Clout	– a blow
Sock	– a blow
Dummel	– stupid
Mommel	– confused, worried
Scrunged up	– not enough room
Gayte, Ghet, Ghut or Gyte	– gate
Hisn, hern	– his, hers
Took to	– astonished
Ruckut	– rubbish
Addled	– rotten egg or person, gone queer in the brain
Fly by night	– someone who did a 'moonlight flit'
Scrawp up	– gather up leaves or rubbish
Clomber	– to climb up a tree or over a fence or gate
Smollock	– fall all of a heap
Scawt	– scawt your boots long the ground
Snoffuly	– head cold
Unkid	– awful
Slosheting	– walking through snow
Her's a cyag magger	– She is a nagging woman
Bofflement	– worried
Fammuld	– famished or hungry
In good fettle	– in good health
Shut of day	– twilight
Dout	– put out (the light)
Showel	– shovel
Varnigh	– very nearly
Flommoxed	– muddled or bothered
Tith	– teeth

DIALECT WORDS AND EXPRESSIONS

Narn	– none
Summut	– something
Twunt	– it won't be
Mumchancing	– day-dreaming or thinking
Traipsin in and out	– walking in and out of home
Allus	– always
Pritnear	– pretty near
Fust	– first
Dimpsey	– getting dark

Wer bist gwine? Gwine! I byent a gwine nower. I be just acoming bäck!
Where are you going? Going! I'm not going anywhere. I'm just coming back!

A rustic poet seeing a gate in one of the Wychwood villages in a very bad state wrote:

> Is this the best ghet a man can affoord
> Hung with a chain and tied with a coord
> Is this the best ghet that goes into the clover
> Neither opens nor shets, and you can't gyet over.

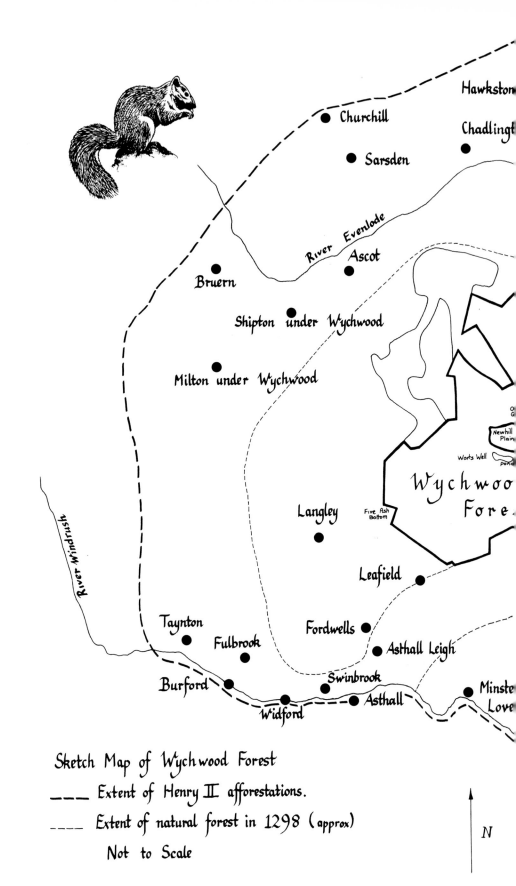

Hawkston

Chadlingt

Churchill

Sarsden

River Evenlode

Ascot

Bruern

Shipton under Wychwood

Milton under Wychwood

Newhill Plain

Worts Well

Wychwoo
Fore.

Five Ash Bottom

Langley

Leafield

River Windrush

Fordwells

Taynton

Fulbrook

Asthall Leigh

Swinbrook

Burford

Minste
Love

Widford

Asthall

Sketch Map of Wychwood Forest

—— Extent of Henry II afforestations.

---- Extent of natural forest in 1298 (approx)

Not to Scale

N

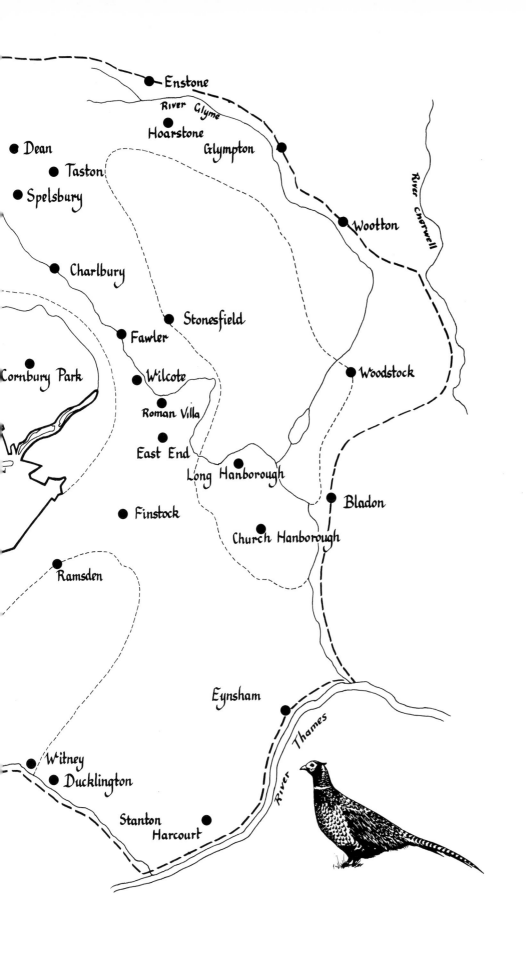

Enstone

River Glyme

Hoarstone

Glympton

Dean

Taston

Spelsbury

River Cherwell

Wootton

Charlbury

Stonesfield

Fawler

Cornbury Park

Wilcote

Woodstock

Roman Villa

East End

Long Hanborough

Finstock

Bladon

Church Hanborough

Ramsden

Eynsham

River Thames

Witney

Ducklington

Stanton Harcourt

n a cold, bleak, January day, Wychwood forest looked, from a distance, dark and foreboding — a huge area of woodland, stark and mysterious. I wondered, as I travelled along, what sort of damage the recent severe gales might have done to the forest trees. There had been a light fall of snow overnight speckling the verge-sides and hedges so that they looked as if they had been sprinkled with icing sugar.

CHAPTER ONE

A

Winter

Walk

in

Wychwood

JANUARY

I slipped into one of the forest openings (having first been given written permission to do so), at Five Ash Bottom, near to Leafield — one of the forest villages. It was quiet and sheltered as I walked along the wide green 'rides' — there were deep water-filled ruts where forest workers had driven along with tractors and land-rovers. Sphagnum moss, vivid green from the recent wet weather, gleamed bright on many of the fallen branches and old tree trunks. And away from the water-filled ruts the ground was covered with grass and soft moss, making my way easy and soft to walk on.

There was much to see on this winter's day; several pheasants who so far had

On the way to Five Ash Bottom

dodged the shooting parties, crossed my path, and here the woodland ground was carpeted with last autumn's leaves, where no doubt the birds were finding plenty to eat.

A hugh flock of starlings wheeled overhead in a wonderful acrobatic flight, probably off to some feeding grounds nearby. And from a spindle-bush, still sporting a few of its bright pinky-orange berries, a solitary bright-eyed robin sang.

Wychwood is the remains of a great royal hunting forest with a wonderful variety of beautiful woodland – oaks, ash, beech, maple and many others, along with lots of scots pines and different conifers.

Along my way there were lots of blackthorn and hawthorn bushes, some with their branches covered in a silvery-

Spindle spray

---

grey lichen. Apparently there are eighty-five different sorts of lichen in Wychwood, several types only to be found there. There were lots of other small bushes, too – privet, guelder rose and dogwood – and already the honey-suckle was showing tight leaf buds, and traveller's joy, or old man's beard, was very prolific with branches as thick as a child's wrist – some of them were climbing up trees and back down again, making the forest, thereabouts, look almost jungle-like. There were also a great many hazel trees and bushes displaying their golden catkins, some were two and a half to three inches long. Taking a closer look, I could see the minute red flowers on the branches – they are pollinated by their own catkins as they swing and sway in the breeze.

Lichen on twigs

I noticed that all along the sides of the grassy rides were little streams, coming out of the banks and trickling along, making their way to the lakes beyond.

Nearby were the remains of a stone cottage, long since deserted. What a lonely life the occupants must have led, for there was no sign of other buildings anywhere, and it must have been a long way from there to any of the villages that skirt Wychwood.

Fallen tree

3

Catkins and marsh tits

A WINTER WALK IN WYCHWOOD
January

Ruined cottage

Having wandered for about two miles along the grassy rides, I came to the first of several ponds, or lakes as they are often called. I have heard that these stretches of water are named after the Great Lakes of Canada, one I understand is called Lake Superior. On this particular day the lake looked calm and still, sheltered by trees of every description – along with brown bracken and blackberry bushes near the water's edge.

Then my walk took me up a steep path. When I reached the top of the hill there were strange cracking and creaking noises, quite loud they were and coming from high up in the branches of some very tall beech trees. It was certainly not the sort of noise that I'd ever heard before. I stopped and peered, wondering what it was – but one thing I hadn't noticed, in the shelter of the forest, was the fact that the wind had got up quite strongly, and the queer noises were the very close branches clanging together high up near the tree-tops. And nearby there were several exceptionally tall scots pines, and the wind was whistling through the top-most branches – yet it was quite sheltered where I was walking.

All over the forest ground in this area was lots of decaying timber, moss-covered, and a wonderful home for beetles and grubs, which in turn will provide food for the birds come spring-time. And by the side of the rotting branches, and sometimes growing on them, were several different sorts of fungi – some I recognized, others I'd never seen before. The ones I did know were the elf cups, earth-stars, wood blewits and tree oysters. There were lovely coloured ones too, – blue, brown, grey,

Great tit and blue tit on fungi

Kennel pond in winter

pinky-orange, cream and white. Not many of them edible – well not as far as I know!

Here and there were newly-fallen trees – victims of the recent gales – and the massive trunks and widespread branches were spread over quite a large area. Some of them had crashed onto standing trees. All this must make a lot of extra work for the foresters. Where the trees had fallen over the rides, great branches had already been sawn off making the rides accessible. A sad sight to see all those magnificent trees – their life ended.

But high up in some nearby trees of maple and beech, life was going on. There were lots and lots of birds, mostly of the tit family, flitting about up there; blue marsh and great tits, and some that I'd never seen before, long-tailed tits. These seemed to be grouped together – apparently the whole family from last year's brood stay in a little family unit, until the offsprings find mates of their own in the spring. The long-tailed tit has some rather odd nicknames, too – long-tailed wanderer, bottle tom, and mum ruffin. I saw some goldcrest, too, and of course lots of pigeons – and there were remnants of their nest still visible from last year.

Victim of the storms

___

But it's time I made my way back on to the roadway and to the nearby village of Leafield where I hope to meet up with a few locals.

The name La Feld is from an early spelling, and means 'A clearing in the Forest', or an open space. The village was first mentioned in 1213, and for centuries was quite remote, until the coming of transport. I remember a woman who had originated from Leafield and who lived next door to us in Ducklington many moons ago, telling of how her father was courting a girl in Witney – some four to five miles away – and used to walk over to see her on Saturday afternoons (having had to work in the morning). He'd stay the night, and then walk back to Leafield on Sunday night, already to be able to start work at 6.30 on Monday morning. There were not many folk in those days who even owned a bike, and there was no other way to get from A to B – or Witney, in his case!

Leafield, a view from the forest

Scots pine

___

Long-tailed tits

 t was nearing the end of the month before I had the chance to walk in Wychwood again. Storms, gales, pouring rain and floods had prevented it. But the last Sunday in the month dawned with a clear blue sky: I knew that underfoot it would be muddy but was determined to go.

Wychwood forest lies about six or seven miles away from my home, so the very pleasant drive through winding country lanes to get there is an added bonus. In the hedgerows some of

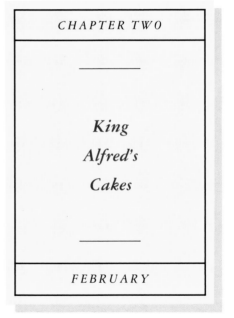

CHAPTER TWO

King
Alfred's
Cakes

FEBRUARY

the early May bushes were already in new green leaf bud – this is surely about a month earlier than usual – and clusters of yellow coltsfoot flowers glowed bright on the verge-sides.

I had arranged to meet Bill (W.D. Campbell) at 10.00 a.m. Bill is a genuine forest man, who lives at nearby Charlbury. His parents brought him to Wychwood when he was five years old and he knows the forest like the back of his hand.

As soon as we entered the vast woodland he pointed out something that I had

On the way to Wychwood from Finstock

never seen before. A special fungi that he called 'King Alfred's cakes' – a very apt name for them because they were just like small round burnt cakes, as black as your hat, and growing on a rotten branch. Bill went on to say that this particular fungi only grows on dead ash wood. Celandines were blooming and a typical woodland plant, dog's mercury, was just about to come out in flower; the shiny leaves of the cuckoo pint (lords and ladies) – some completely green and some with brown splodges – were pushing their way through the forest floor.

It was sheltered and very peaceful as we wandered down those wide grassy rides. I remarked on the vast amount of lichen that was growing on many of the trees – whether they were still growing, or the fallen ones. Bill said that lichen only grows where the air is pure – and pure it was, and I savoured it like old wine and felt very privileged to be able to walk in that lovely forest.

'See these trees,' my companion said, 'they are rather special and are called hedge

---

maples, but as you can see they are quite tall trees and at least 250 years old, and in another part of the forest there is, in fact, the biggest hedge maple in the British Isles.' 'Anyhow,' he went on, 'the reason these trees were grown in the first place was the fact that it is a very hard wood, and in the twelfth and thirteenth centuries the reigning kings had drinking vessels, dishes and plates made from the hedge maple, and apparently the drinking vessels were called mazers.'

There was quite a variety of colour from the trees and bushes. Golden catkins on the hazels still showed up in groups of yellow, but the larches were of a more fawny shade, not having yet lost last year's spikey leaves; even the humble blackthorn bushes looked almost wine-red in the sunshine.

And under the bushes at this particular spot we found empty Roman snail shells. They are much bigger than the ordinary ones and a lovely creamy colour with darker bands around them. Apparently these snails hibernate mostly down old rabbit holes, then, having found a comfortable place to spend the winter, they seal their shell entrance with a thick limey substance (quite different to the ordinary snail) which keeps them warm and dry until spring. We could hear a few gunshots:

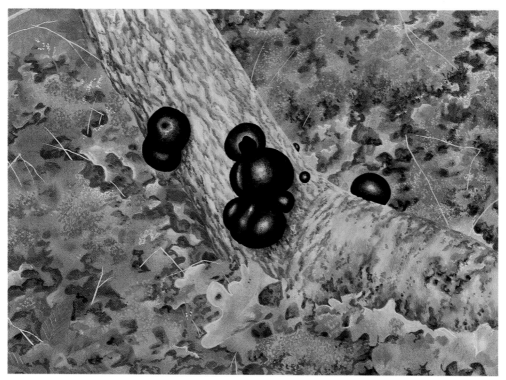

King Alfred's cakes growing on trunk of dead ash

13

Hedge maple

'I expect they are having a vermin shoot,' Bill said. 'I know all about vermin shoots,' I replied, 'I went on one years ago' –

A bubbling spring appeared from a high bank along the ride. It is called Worts Well (Wort being the old-fashioned word for healing). To the locals it is called Wassel, but in the old days it was pronounced 'Ussel' or 'Uzzel'.

USSEL, UZZEL OR WORTS WELL

Hast then a wound to heal
The Wych doth grieve thee
Come then unto this well
It will relieve thee:
Nolie me tangeries,*
And other maladies
Have here thyr remedies
Pray'sd be the Lord.

Early man felt that God was near a spring, it was Wych, and the wood containing it was Wychwood. Man believed that the waters in Wychwood had healing properties. Probably on account of there being iron in the water.

And it was from this well, or spring, that many years ago the folk from Leafield (the nearest

Medieval mazers

* I wondered what this line meant. One day I was looking through a very old book called *Flowers of the Field* when I came across the following: *Impatiens* (Balsam) *noli-me-tangere*, called 'Touch me not' and 'impatient' because of the sudden curling of the valves of the capsule which, when touched, instantly sprinkles its seeds by the way.

WYCHWOOD
The Secret Cotswold Forest

Wassel stream

village), and others surrounding the forest, used to collect water in bottles on Spanish Liquor Day. Now, people walk right down to the lakes or wells. Worts Well goes on to trickle for almost a mile, getting wider and deeper until it finally flows into Withy pond at Withy Bottom. And here in that clear spring

Muntjäc deer

water several different plants grow — brilliant green marestail and water star, and many others.

A little further on was another stretch of water, this was Newel pond. Here on the water's edge grew several bushes, but the one that showed up more than the others was the dogwood — bright pinky-red, reflecting in the water; a pair of tufted ducks, startlingly black and white, rose up and flew overhead. I could see lots of deer slots; this is what the marks made from their hooves are called. Then I noticed some much smaller ones. 'Are these from young deer?' I enquired. 'No,' Bill said, 'they are marks made by wild muntjäc deer, and if you notice,' he went on, 'one toe mark is always shorter than the other!'

We walked on to The Grand Vista, a lovely long stretch of grassland flanked on both sides with magnificent trees. We turned round, and from there could see Cornbury Mansion. Near the house is a gate called 'The Vista Gate', but years and years ago the locals did not know what Vista meant and always called it 'The Bister Gayte' — they knew that the town of Bicester was fairly near, and thought that was what it referred to. Then we walked on to Newel Plain over to the forest edge.

Roman snails and pick which was used to hook out and eat the snails

Buzzard, a welcome sight in the forest

Tufted duck, dogwood and water weed

Suddenly Bill said, 'Look! a pair of buzzards. I haven't seen any in here for ages. I just hope they will nest here.' The pair of huge birds flew over our heads and into the thickness of the forest.

'Here's something I'll bet you've never seen before,' Bill said, as he wandered over to a lovely old oak tree. It was oak fern, and growing inbetween the branches was a dark, big-leafed fern, which was very unusual.

Then we came to a scrubby area. From a distance the bronze leaves on some short bushy trees looked like beech. 'No,' Bill said, 'they are turkey oaks, and a blessed nuisance they are too. Whereas not many acorns from ordinary oaks grow, everyone from the turkey oaks do,' and he picked up a 'cup' that had held an acorn. That was different, too, for it was covered in small thistley prickles. And everywhere there were mosses – dozens of different sorts grow here, on the ground and on the masses of fallen branches, some which are completely covered making

Rare oak fern

them look like families of greeny reptiles, crawling and winding over the forest floor. Some mosses had also sprawled up some of the tree trunks, noticeably on the north side. And it is said that on dark nights poachers could find out which direction they were walking simply by feeling around moss-covered trees.

Turkey oak

We made our way back out of the forest at Five Ash Bottom. Very reluctantly I said cheerio to Bill Campbell. It had been a most enlightened walk, and he had shown me where I could walk and the things to observe during the coming months of 1990.

On my way home I had promised to call on a retired head-keeper Bill Whittington, in the hope that he might be able to tell me some poaching stories.

'Well,' he said, 'only once during many years of keepering did I come across one case, and this happened about ten years ago.' He went on, 'One night, I had a 'phone call from one of my keepers to say that he had heard some gunshots in the forest near his home, and he had had a walk around, but couldn't see anyone. So I hopped in my truck and drove over there. We walked about, but couldn't see a sign of anybody. Just as we were about to give up, I noticed something white under a bush. Without a word to my keeper I took a running dive and landed on a couple of fellows hiding there – AND they'd

Snake-like branches

21

got a couple of pheasants, too. The cunning devils had left their car right up in the village of Leafield, nearly a mile away. It appeared that they were a couple of undergrads from Oxford. I drove them to Chipping Norton Police Station, and then in a few days they came up before the magistrate – and got off!'

What a difference, I thought. In October 1878 Philip Moss and Edward Pratley of Leafield were captured and convicted at Chipping Norton for poaching in the forest at Priest Grove (probably because their families were starving). They were sentenced to one month's imprisonment and sureties for one year or six months in prison, and they were also fined for carrying guns without a licence.

Beech   *Larch*

arch came in like a lamb and during the month we had balmy, spring-like days along with a few frosts at night. In the two weeks since I last visited Wychwood there were many different things to see. In clear parts the forest floor was speckled with violets and primroses. There were also several clumps of daffodils – but I wasn't sure if these were of the wild variety originally. It was around this area that I noticed some very different fungi: it wasn't until I was allowed to

CHAPTER THREE

———

Razor
Strops
and
Jew's Ears

———

MARCH

walk in Wychwood that I realized that there were so many different types. On some rotten silver birch was a very thick growth which looked like scallop shells: I discovered that they were called 'razor strops'; then on some dead elder I noticed some small brownish cap-like fungi, quite soft – these are called 'Jew's ears'; yet another I came across was flattish but a lovely colour – deep creamy with orange and brown markings – these had the strange name of 'bracket'. Of course, when the trees and bushes are covered with leaves, the dead branches where most of the fungi grows will be obscured, so I am glad that I noticed them during the early months of the year.

———

Primrose, a prolific early forest flower

The sober black of winter was already disappearing from Wychwood, the top-most branches of the huge beech trees were a delicate shade of pink, and the willow branches – some red, some yellow, some amber and some still with soft yellow pussy willow on them showed up here and there. And the snowy-white black-thorn and wild cherry blossom tumbled everywhere, and several brimstone butterflies were flying around.

Suddenly out of the bushes a very tiny bird flew, followed by its mate. They were, in fact, a pair of goldcrest, or goldcrested wren, and the smallest bird in Great Britain. I suspect they were searching for material to build their nest with – probably in a nearby pine tree. I have only ever once seen a goldcrest's nest. Many moons ago one of my brothers showed me one. It was like a miniature hammock suspended between small branches. It was made of moss, spiders' webs and lichen. The brood had already left and my brother showed me the inside of this work of art – it was half-filled with downy feathers and must have taken those tiny birds days and days to make.

On one of the lakes, so calm and beautiful in the spring sunshine, there was quite a large flock of mallard and on some swampy ground nearby I noticed some most peculiar plants growing. They were clusters of brownish rhizomes just emerging from the damp ground. I found out that they were called 'marestails' or 'water horsetails' and are one of the oldest surviving plants, reputed to be 200 million years old. Apparently dinosaurs used to eat them. The leaves of the horsetails are very gritty to the touch and contain silica and, before the days of pan-scourers, were used for cleaning pots and pans.

As I walked down the wide green rides I was trying to

Violets

24

Jew's ears, fungi on dead elder

First of the season brimstone butterfly

imagine what this once royal forest must have looked like when the kings of England hunted there – probably much the same as it did today, although of course it does not cover such a wide area as it did in the sixteenth century when King Henry VIII hunted there: he was very fond of hunting, especially with Anne Boleyn, who was herself a great sportswoman, joining in the hunt and also shooting with the bow and arrow. They often stayed at nearby Langley, a hunting lodge, which King John had built: it was known as Langley Palace, and some remains of it are still visible, although it is now just a farmhouse. But what a picture Henry and Anne must have made as they rode

horse-back from London to Oxford-shire with their entourage of dozens of noblemen, friends and servants, with the elaborate decorations of brasses and adornments of the horses (one of Anne's saddles cost £4.10, and had tassles of gold and silver on it – in those days, a farm labourer only earned about eight shillings a week). Then there was the colourful dress of the King and his noblemen. And what great preparations would have had to be made for such a journey for so many people to stay at mansions on the way. It is said that King Henry and his followers once killed two hundred deer in one day. What feasting the whole court must have had with all that venison to consume.

Razor strops, unusual fungi

Goldcrest, the smallest British bird, on blackthorn

As I stood wondering which path to take, five or six fallow deer came down to a nearby lake to drink at the water's edge. Suddenly every head went up, they had heard something – probably me – in a flash they were gone, disappearing into some thickets nearby. Seeing them reminded me of a story I heard once. There was this man from the Wychwood area who had shot a deer; he lifted it up and hung it around his neck with the legs hanging down each side, which he held on to. As he neared his home he felt the animal move slightly. He had, in fact, only wounded it. Suddenly the deer struggled and caught one of its feet in the man's trouser pocket; still struggling, the animal tore the trousers from top to bottom and, with a leap, was gone deep into the forest.

Well, the other day I called to see retired head game-keeper, Bill Archer, and his wife. Bill had worked in Swinbrook village for many years and Swinbrook was once part of Wychwood. They lived in a 600-year-old cottage at Furzy Leys. The cottage had once been the home of King Charles II's head-groom, and at the back were a

WYCHWOOD

The Secret Cotswold Forest

Lake Superior and mallard

few remains where the stables had once been. Apparently the King used to hold races in the valley thereabouts. The estate where Bill had worked for many years was heavily-wooded and he was responsible for arranging the big shoots for his employer. A few years ago another woman and I went 'beating' for Bill. We arrived on the scene – having never done this job before – and there were about fifteen men and we two. Bill looked at us and then shouted to the rest, 'They got no bloody sticks,' and promptly went over to the hedge and cut us one apiece. You see, we beaters who were very well organized by the head-keeper had to 'beat out' the pheasants by whacking the tree trunks and bushes with

King Henry VIII

our sticks to scare the birds in the direction of the 'guns'. The shoot was planned like an army manoeuvre and Bill had to keep us 'in line' well away from the guns. After we had beaten one big wood we would all pile into land-rovers and drive over to another part of this very large estate. Bill used to swear at us if we got out of line and his loud voice shouting, 'Keep in bloody line,' echoed through the woods all day. After that first day's 'beating' my friend and I were asked to go on many others, on different estates in the neighbourhood, and a couple of times we went to Cornbury when Mr Bill Whittington was head-keeper there. Then, at the end of the game-shooting season, we were asked if we would like to go on a vermin shoot. The 'guns' were head-keepers and under-keepers from other estates along with the Corn-bury ones. During that cold March day the men

Anne Boleyn

killed several hares, rabbits, squirrels, pigeons magpies and jays. At the end of the day these were all carefully laid out in rows and we beaters could choose something from there.

I chose three jays. 'What are you going to do with them?' one of the keepers asked. 'Have 'um stuffed,' I replied.

I had fairly recently interviewed a farm worker from Glympton who had taught himself to stuff animals and birds and had become quite an experienced taxidermist. So, I took the jays to him and he made a wonderful job of them, setting them on a branch with moss and twigs around, but using just two of the birds as one was badly knocked about. People who see them in their glass case on my sideboard think that they are really old. They are a constant reminder of that rather special day.

But now Bill has retired, 'Well I does a bit of gardening,' he told me, 'just to keep me out of bloody mischief.' 'Did you have many poachers on the estate?' I asked him. 'No bloody fear! I used to make it known when I went to the pub that if I ever caught one I'd pepper his ass with my shot-gun. And them as heard me say that knew that I meant it, so they took particular notice that they kept off my territory.'

Bill Archer

'What about that time you missed that fox?' his wife asked.

'Well,' Bill went on, 'I'd been after this old devil for ages – they says as cunning as a fox and this 'un was certainly a cunning old bugger. Anyhow, one day I was out looking for him, course I'd got me gun "broken" for safety. Then I saw him in the distance. Quickly I climbed over a gate and "cocked" me gun, but that old sod

Fallow deer

Marestails, survivors from the past

heard me. He turned, and looked at me and give a sly grin, and in a second was off into the bushes, before I could fire at him. I was in such a bloody temper to think I'd bin so near and he'd got away, I grabs me hat off me head and chucked it up in the air and fired at that – peppered with holes it was, too.'

'Course, Bill loves his beer, I reckon thats what keeps him going.' His wife said, 'When his maker calls for him and says, "Now, William, its time for you to go," if he's got a pint in his hand he'll say, "well, you just wait till I've finished this, I 'ent leaving this behind."'

What a marvellous pair! I promised to call and see them again very soon.

Time I made my way home. There was so much small rotted wood lying about in the forest – what I call 'kindling wood'. It seems nowadays nobody exercises their 'wooding rights', which have existed for hundreds of years. People living in the villages that skirt the forest are allowed to pick and carry away fallen wood in their arms – but no wheeled vehicles are allowed in there. Folk from each village were given a special half day when they could do this. I know that Leafield's half day is on a Tuesday, and Ramsden and Finstock on a Thursday, but I must find out as I go along about the other villages.

Well, now it is the last day of March, the month came in like a lamb – so we country folk thought that it would go out like a lion, that's the old saying anyhow – BUT not this year! The temperature over much of the country was in the late sixties and seventies, brilliant sunshine all day, butterflies and honey bees in the garden, and the garden flowers quite a month earlier than usual.

The old 'uns will say, 'We shall have to pay for this,' and maybe we shall get some cold weather yet. But, remembering something that Bill Archer's wife told me, something that Bill's granny had told her years ago, 'Thee wunt knwaw one season from 'tuther affore the end of the world' – well, it's getting a bit like that now.

Bill shooting his cap

'e you goin' down tu the Forest come Sunday?' an elderly lady asked me, many years ago.

CHAPTER FOUR

—

*Spanish
Liquor
and
Blackthorn
Winter*

—

APRIL

'Forest? What forest?' I enquired.

'Well, Wychwood forest, a course', she replied. 'It's Liquorice Sunday, we allus goes down thur on Palm Sunday,' she went on, 'Do you mean tu tell me as you've lived in Oxfordshire all your life and you 'ent never heard of it?'

I had to admit that I hadn't.

She said that it was an old custom that is still kept up in the Wychwood forest, and it is called Spanish Sunday, or Spanish Liquor Day, and it always falls on Palm Sunday. And this is the only day in the year that the public are allowed in this once royal forest – unless you get a special permit for bird-watching. She told me that when she was young they never missed going, as she only lived a couple of miles from the forest, and on the Saturday night before, they always got their bottles ready. The idea of going to the forest was so that you could fill your bottle up with the magic water that flowed there.

Just before the great day, her mother would buy a lump of real black liquorice

33

Worts Well, locally known as Ussel or Uzzel

Blossom and cones on larch branch

from an old lady in the village; she would chop it up and give all her family a piece to put in their bottles, along with that they would put a spoonful of brown sugar and a black peppermint, and then they hung the bottles up in a myrtle bush all Saturday night to keep witches away.

Then the next morning they were up early and all the village children would trail down to the forest. Once there they had to walk another two miles before they reached the lakes, ponds, or wells — as some people call them. And when they reached the biggest stretch of water — that the locals call Lake Superior, they would dip their bottles in and fill them up.

If you drank this concoction it was supposed to cure anything that you had wrong with you.

The old lady also told me that one old fellow used to declare that the water contained iron, so I suppose that was why folks started to drink it, and the sweets were most likely added later to make it taste better. Of course, these days people can get all the medicine they want through the National Health, but years ago folk used herbs and things for their illnesses. It was only the rich who could afford to have a doctor visit them.

This chat with the old lady happened over thirty years ago, and I have been going down to the forest to the wells on Palm Sunday ever since. I buy my liquorice from the chemist, but when I met Mr Sheasby — who, together with his late wife have done a complete survey of all the flowers and trees that grow in Wychwood — he pointed out a

Frog

WYCHWOOD

The Secret Cotswold Forest

Spring scene

Blackbird

very rough sort of tufty grass that he told me was a liquorice plant, and he thought that in the first instance, centuries ago, people *might* have used the root from this plant – perhaps before the real black Spanish liquorice was available to them.

Another thing that both Mr Sheasby and naturalist, Bill Campbell, pointed out to me in the forest was the original well, but this is not where folk go nowadays. It really is a lovely spring, falling out of the hillside, not far from one of the entrances to the forest. Its proper name is Worts Well. Mr Sheasby thought that the word Wort was something to do with healing, like the old herbs are – such as liver wort and hound wort. But, through the centuries the name for the well has become Wassel, although the old 'uns called it Ussel or Uzzel. And, the water from Worts Well flows on for about two miles before it joins one of the lakes.

For many years I used to drink my Spanish liquor like the old folks did, but not anymore. One year as I was dipping my bottle into one of the lakes, I noticed dozens and dozens of frogs in there. That did it! I still carry my bottle and fill it up – but that's all.

And it was near Wassel this month that I saw one of the buzzards that I first spotted in February. The huge bird was being mobbed by a crow. As I only saw one buzzard it may mean that its mate is sitting on eggs. I do hope so, as I understand it is several years since a pair have nested there.

There was a great difference in the forest

Ladybirds

since I last paid a visit which was about three weeks ago. Many of the trees – beech, maple, hawthorn and poplar, were all showing new delicate green buds, and on some, yellow catkins were spreading their pollen

Wren among the fungi and blackberry leaves

in tiny clouds. I even saw a May bush in full flower – quite a month earlier than usual. And the very bright green of the new larch spikes ran like a ribbon through the tree-tops. Some of the lower branches still had last year's cones on them, but what was so beautiful was that the branches were also covered with lovely rose-pink flowers which, of course, will eventually become this year's cones.

I came across a very old flat stump of a tree: it must have been the remains of a huge tree for it was eight to ten feet in diameter. Places like this are wonderful for wild life of all sorts. As I stood gazing at the old stump, out flitted a little wren, probably after the larvae that winter there. And the lovely warm sun was encouraging several ladybirds to emerge from the cracks. There was also some fungi growing from the wood, a type that I had not seen before. Blackberry bramble grew around – still showing last year's leaves (these usually stay on until the new ones push them off in the spring). And red admiral and brimstone butterflies flew around there, and a male blackbird, most likely because I was near his nest, was chacketting away angrily. He is called 'The policeman of the woods', because he warns the other birds of danger – in this case a human. Then I walked on to Vista Plain where I saw several welcome clumps of cowslips, and near the forest edge delicate anemones (wind flowers) were growing alongside masses of bluebells.

Chrysomela beetle

It was warm and sheltered in the forest, but for the first three weeks of this month we have had cold winds and disastrous frosts along with hail and a little snow. Yet, in March we had several summer-like days with very high temperatures in the sixties and even seventy degrees Fahrenheit on one day, which encouraged everything to grow like billyho, and I began to think that what my granny always called 'Blackthorn Winter' – a period of cold winds and frosts when the blackthorn is out – was not, for the first time in my lifetime, going to come about. But, her old prediction was right after all: those first three weeks of this month were proof enough. And those unusual horsetail plants that I wrote about last month had really taken a hammering from the frost, and some would probably not recover – especially the more advanced ones. But the wild mint had stood up to the hard weather alright. I can never resist squeezing the leaves between finger and thumb, it is such a fresh spring smell. In this particular area, big clumps of wood spurge were growing, their green flowers like miniature saucers. That is what is so fascinating about the forest: I keep coming across wondrous plants,

Red admiral on wood spurge

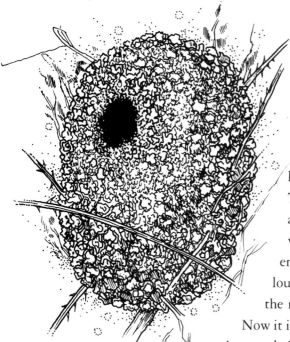

Long-tailed tit's nest

some of which only grow in certain places – like the wood spurge – for I had not come across it before. And down by the lake's edge, a clump of strange-looking fern was growing. I shall have to look it up in Mr Sheasby's records to see if I can identify it. And the moist ground there was covered in very small irridescent, kingfisher blue and mauvy-green, beetles. They are apparently called chrysomela beetles and the lovely colours are something to do with their physical structure. At the other end of the lake a pair of Canada geese honked loudly at my presence, and then nearby I found the ruins of what had been an old pump-house. Now it is a cool, fern-like grotto with trickling water here and there. I had approached it very quietly, and suddenly disturbed six or eight lovely fallow deer who had been drinking there in that beautiful secluded spot.

I had hoped to find a long-tailed tit's nest on this day – I am sure they should be nesting there by now – and I kept peering into blackthorn bushes thinking I might catch sight of one. I was within five hundred yards of the gate and the roadway and had given up all hope of finding one . . . when, suddenly, there was a flutter from out of the thicket. Sure enough, it was a long-tailed tit. I gazed into the thick bush from where the bird had emerged, and there it was, a lovely nest built in the middle of the bush and definitely so deep in the thickness of it that no way could anything but the birds reach it. But I could clearly see this wonderful nest: it was quite four inches long, sort of dome-shaped, like a very small marrow, and hung delicately on the

Canada goose

twigs. I could see bits of wool, green moss and lichen on it – they evidently use the lichen to make the nest water-tight.

Now the long-tailed tit had returned, so I crept away so as not to frighten it, and made my way, quite happily, home.

The old pump-house

'All in a rush of richness' – that is how someone once described the month of May, and how true it was. It seemed that magically overnight flowers were wide out and the trees in full leaf. Along the country roads from my home in Eynsham to Wychwood, the verge-sides were shoulder high with cow parsley (called kek in my neck of the woods), and the blossom on the May bushes was so heavy that the branches were bowed down with their weight – simply dripping with the heady flowers so that they looked as if they were covered with snow. You can make a lovely light wine with these flowers which captures the very essence of spring. The elder blossom was full out, too, and of course wine and champagne can be made from these.

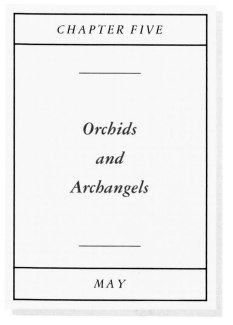

Orchids
and
Archangels

MAY

I was driving slowly through one of the villages that skirt the forest when I noticed in one countryman's garden a 'tater 'awk swinging in the breeze. You don't see many of them about these days, no doubt being near to Wychwood the gardener is plagued with birds from there. But he's not the only one to make these

Blackcap on elder blossom

bird-scarers, because each year about this time I make myself a couple of 'tater 'awks.

Strangers, especially townsfolk, who come to live in the houses that skirt my vegetable garden, gaze in wonderment at these feathered contraptions swinging in the breeze.

I got the habit of making them from my gramp. He and my gran lived in a lodge cottage that skirted Sherborne Park in the Cotswolds. And living, as they did, on the edge of the great park, their garden was always at the mercy of hordes of woodland birds, and the only thing that scared them off were his 'tater 'awks.

Every springtime he would say, 'Ah, 'tis time I had a word with old Nathan [he was head-keeper on the Sherborne estate] and ask him if he'll shoot I a sparrow 'awk or two.'

Then, having got his feathers he'd get a few nobbly potatoes – they had to be nobbly so that he could tie a piece of string round them. Then the largest feathers from the sparrow hawks were stuck into the potatoes, making a good tail and outspread wings, and looking quite lifelike.

Then these feathered contraptions were hung on a piece of string about a yard long and tied on to a stick, which was pushed into the ground at a slight angle, leaving the 'tater 'awk swinging and twirling at the slightest breeze. Mind you, I don't use sparrow hawks feathers! No, I usually use some from the cock pheasants that come my way during the shooting season, but

'Tater 'awk

43

Early purple orchid

this year I picked lots up in Wychwood. And the 'awks certainly do the trick. They keep the birds from pecking at the spring cabbage, then through the summer they keep them off the rows of peas and summer cabbage, right on to the autumn, when the young plants of the winter greens are growing – the finest bird-scarer I've ever seen.

As I approached the forest on this perfect May day, Wychwood looked beautiful. The trees were displaying every shade of green imaginable – so different from the foreboding look of January and February when the only green was that of the conifers which, anyway, were now almost lost in that great forest.

Tudor ruff

This month I was eager to find some early orchids. Mr Sheasby, whom I had met earlier in the year, said to look for the first ones in May before the deer eat the blossoms off. I suppose they find them nice and sweet, as well as a change of diet. I hadn't been walking long – guided by Mr Sheasby's map – before I found a clump of early purple-spotted orchids in full flower, and lots of another variety in big tight buds which should be out in full flower in a couple of weeks time I would think. It was while I was searching for the orchids that I remembered a story that Bill Campbell had told me one day when I met him in Wychwood. It happened one spring when he, too, was looking out for those first orchids in this self-same spot. He told me, 'I noticed in the grass a little to my left what looked like a dead hen pheasant with its wings spread out. Poor devil, I thought, I

Comfrey

wonder what killed it. As I bent to get a good look at the orchids I noticed a slight movement – perhaps it had been injured and I should put it out of its misery. I walked towards the bird, it wasn't a dying pheasant but a very live woodcock feigning death to put me off going near its nest which held a couple of chicks – I retreated very quickly, not wishing to disturb it any more than I already had.'

There were several different flowers out since I last walked in Wychwood – yellow archangels, lady's bedstraw and a lovely clump of pink herb robert growing in the crevice of a tree trunk. And the hazy blue of millions of bluebells under the trees is always a welcome spring sight.

I discovered that in the Elizabethan Age, when those huge white ruffs were the fashion for both men and women, that they were kept stiff and white by using the bulbs of bluebells and orchids, which are full of starch – until now I did wonder how they kept them looking so crisp and white.

There were several big clumps of comfrey plants with their little bell-like flowers of pink and blue on the same stalks. When I take my dog, Sally, for her morning

Woodcock and chicks, beautifully camouflaged

Carpet of bluebells, a haze in the forest

walk we pass masses of them growing on the verge-side. I always pick a spray of them and lay a few leaves under the tomato plants in the greenhouse; this keeps the dreaded whitefly away. And some leaves laid on the compost heap do wonders to kill off all sorts of pests that will lurk there to lay their eggs – to trouble us next season. In the old days, an infusion of leaves in hot water was good for sufferers of bronchitis and colds. However, present day scientists say that they are poisonous.

The chestnut trees simply dripped with blossom: Whitsuntide candles is the country name for them, but methinks they will be gone over come Whitsuntide. And very noticeable was the new growth on the fir trees, about a couple of inches there was of bright green young spikes. Underneath were hundreds of huge fir cones about four or five inches long they were. Butterflies were everywhere on this heavenly day, such a lot of the small orange-tipped ones, and a pair which I actually saw mating on the head of a gone-to-seed dandelion. Country names for dandelions range from 'blow-a-clocks' – children used to blow them off and chant, 'one o'clock, two o'clock,' and so on until all the seeds had gone – to dandidick, old man's clock and four-a-clock. In days gone by, the milky sap from the dandelion stalk was used to cure

Archangels and herb robert

Fir cone

warts simply by rubbing the wart daily until it disappeared. There were also a few meadow brown butterflies and cabbage white, which are a common sight in my garden, anyhow.

I didn't catch sight of the buzzards this time, but the place was full of wood pigeons. We always say that their call sounds like 'My toes bleed Betty', 'Coo-coo, coo-cooeee!' Others say it sounds like 'Not tonight, Flora', and 'My foot hurts Pauline'. But whatever it is they were in full song. I also caught sight of a pair of green woodpeckers, these were in the conifer area. And there were lots of blue tits and blackcaps flying around.

Long ago there was an old custom whereby at Whitsuntide certain people were allowed to hunt and kill deer in Wychwood forest. Nearby, the townsfolk of Witney were allowed to kill three – the first went to the village of Hailey, the second to Crawley and the third to Witney town. In each of these places the animals were roasted in the street and a good feed was had by all. And in the town of Bampton, (the old name was Bampton-in-the-Bush) which in the early days was also part of Wychwood, the townsfolk were also allowed to kill a deer on Whit Monday. The animal was cut up and carried round the place accompanied by the morris dancers, and pieces were given to the locals. Now, the morris men still start their season of dancing on Whit Monday, and instead of carrying around venison, as they did in the old days, one of the dancers has a tin fixed on his hat or on a pole which contains a rich fruit cake, and pieces of this are given away to the locals. Mr Francis Shergold, who has been connected with the famous Bampton morris men all his life says that this is the origin of the Whitsuntide festivities, which these days attract crowds of people to Bampton. And the Bampton Morris Team have danced all over the world.

I came across the following account of the Whit Hunt, which is about the village of Ducklington; having lived there for many years I'd never heard about this event connected with the village of my youth.

Wood pigeon

'I have selected the village of Ducklington, about two miles south of Witney, as typical of the surrounding district. At the hour of midnight on Whit Sunday, the villagers were roused from their sleep, by the blowing of "peeling horns", and the loud shouts of their bearers, to prepare for the coming festivities. These "peeling horns" were made of green willow-bark, peeled in a long spiral strip from a bough previously well soaked and beaten, in

Orange-tipped butterflies mating on a gone-to-seed dandelion

order to loosen the bark. This strip was then rolled up in a long funnel shape, about 11 inches long, and 2½ inches in diameter at the larger end. To the smaller end was fitted a reed, about 2 inches long, made of willow-bark stripped from a twig without any incision being made in it. This reed was called the "trumpet". The edges of the reed, which entered the mouth of the player, were pinched closely together to produce the sound. The whole horn was pinned together with the long thorns of the blackthorn.

'At daybreak on the Monday, all the men of the village who could beg or borrow a horse, rode off to the village of Hailey on the edge of the forest, where they were joined by a crowd of hunters from the surrounding towns and villages of Witney, Bampton, Brize Norton, Crawley, Leafield, Charlbury, Finstock, etc. The crowd then moved off in a body, and proceeded to chase and kill three deer, one of which was claimed by Hailey, one by Crawley, and one by Witney, the first-named having always the prior claim. The man who was first in at the death of the deer claimed the head and antlers as his trophy, and the antlers seem to have been kept for years after as a mark of distinction. The carcass of the deer was then carried in triumph to an inn, where it was skinned. The skin was cut up into pieces, and distributed, and happy was the maiden whose

Horse chestnut (Whitsuntide candles)

lover could sport a piece of skin in his cap, for it brought good luck and ensured her marriage within the coming year. This ceremony was discontinued some fifty years ago.'

This was written by W.J. Monk in 1894. Another little piece of local history also came my way. From Ashford Mill, which is situated in the parish of Northleigh (once part of Wychwood forest), comes this nursery rhyme that dates back to Charles II's reign in 1660:

> Lucy Locket lost her pocket
> Kitty Fisher found it.
> Took it down to Ashford Mill
> And Ashford Miller ground it.

(Ashford Mill is still standing, though it is no longer a flour mill.)

Green woodpecker

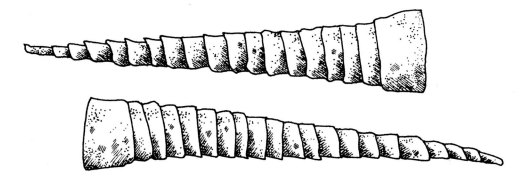

'Peeling horns', made in Ducklington 1897

y June visit to Wychwood forest happened a few days after we'd had several good downpours of rain – the first for many weeks.

Whereas the countryside all over had begun to look very dry and dusty, today it seemed like a different world, and as I entered the Secret Forest on this perfect summer day, every tree, bush, flower and blade of grass simply glistened – all had been revived by the recent storms and it looked like an Amazon forest. The growth of every-

CHAPTER SIX

*Aspen Trees
and
Deadly
Nightshade*

JUNE

thing was fantastic, and it wasn't long before I found two different species of lovely wild orchid – the early purple and spotted. No wonder they are called 'the precious stones of the forest', rare and beautiful as they are. There were some different types still in tight bud, but I'll have to check with Mr Sheasby's list to find out which variety they are. The only ones I remember, from the days of my youth, are the type that we called blue butchers – which we crudely named 'bloody butchers'.

There was a most wonderful selection of wild flowers in bloom – rosebay,

Midsummer in Wychwood

'Tittybottles' (country name for campion)

willowherb, foxgloves, blue meadow cranesbill, rock roses, poppies, pink and white campion (we always called them 'tittybottles' because that's what they look like!), moon daisies, red dead nettle and dog roses, were just a few that were at their best. And sweet-smelling honeysuckle trailed and climbed everywhere – I stopped to look closely at a group of ramson flowers, they are quite rare in my neck of the woods, but here, undisturbed, they were growing profusely. Above me I could hear a soft rustling, yet there was hardly a breath of air along the sheltered rides: I knew in a flash what it was – an aspen tree. The stalks are so thin that the leaves are agitated by the least little breeze, and they flutter and make a delightful sound. And in my mind I was back in the home of my childhood in Ducklington, remembering something our next-door-neighbour had said, all those years ago. Her only daughter had had a very bad fright, and missus-next-door was telling our mother about it . . . "er shook like a tree full of Hasspen leaves 'er did.' (She would put H's where there were none, and drop them where they should have been.) Of course, our parents tried desperately to make us speak properly, and we'd snigger at missus-next-door's funny chatter: but one look from our mother soon stopped that, and afterwards we each got a clout round the ear for laughing at the poor old soul.

And in Wales at one time the folk believed in the

Yellow flags

Wassal (Ussel) flowing on to Withy pond

legend that the leaves were restless and would never be still, because Christ was crucified on a cross made from aspen wood.

But an expression our mother used when the aspen leaves were blowing and showing their silvery-white undersides, was, 'When the aspen tree is showing her petticoats that's a sure sign of rain,' and something that I still believe in to this day.

I wandered down the green ride and gradually the stream from the spring called Wassel (or Ussel – as some of the locals call it), was getting much wider and soon flowed into Withy pond, then on a little further to Kennel pond (these are lakes really). Bill Campbell told me that he always knew Kennel pond as the Trout Lake and he always calls it that. In an earlier chapter, I spoke of finding the horse or marestails when they first came up out of the ground, well, now they are about three or four feet high and very thick on the uneven ground over quite a large area along by the ruined cottage; there was a slight breeze coming off the lake and the mass of pale green horsetails looked like a green, wavy sea.

On the lake (Kennel) there were swans, moorhen and coot – all with young families. Some people have difficulty in telling the difference between moorhens and coot: the coot is the one with the white patch on the front of its head, hence the expression 'as bald as a coot'. There were big clumps of yellow flag flowers around the edges of the lake, and in among the tall sword-like leaves were three or four moorhen nests; here some of the leaves were very cleverly bent over the nests to make a covering, almost like a little roof, to shade the youngsters from the sun or rain. There were several different sorts of rushes growing there, too, some with greeny-brown flowers on them. When these rushes were split open and peeled, what was left was a stalk of white pith. This was dipped in tallow fat and used for lighting purposes, and known as *rush* lights – a far cry from the electric lights of today.

And, joy of joys! high above me one of the buzzards was flying and circling, so I would imagine that its mate was either busy sitting on eggs or looking after their youngsters somewhere high in the trees. I stopped to

Rushes

Coot with her young on nest

WYCHWOOD
The Secret Cotswold Forest

Underside of buzzard in flight

look at what I would think is the biggest, oldest beech tree in Wychwood – maybe three hundred years old. Then, suddenly a little treecreeper scampered up the trunk: they are quite difficult to spot as they are the self-same colour of tree bark.

I didn't catch sight of any deer on this walk, but then, this is the month when the females have their fawns, and maybe the dutiful males are staying near at hand. But a muntjäk, which is a species of small wild deer rushed across my path, and disappeared in a flash.

Patches of bracken had suddenly grown tall and straight, and looked like soldiers on parade. Bracken is really a menace and spreads very quickly, but I suppose it provides cover for the pheasants. I only saw a few cock pheasants and a group of seven young ones, about ten or twelve weeks old I would think, but obviously old enough to fend for themselves.

Then I walked down the green ride to beautiful Lake Superior – it was so still and lovely, and here again there was much wild life, swimming and diving for food. There were several huge patches of both white and yellow water lilies on there: we used to call the yellow ones 'goosey ganders'. Another country name for them is 'brandy bottles' because the shape of the flower resembles one. Around the lake, quite a lot of deadly nightshade was growing; the plants were covered with biggish, purply, bell-like flowers, and although poisonous it is used medicinally as a heart

Deadly nightshade

Camouflaged treecreepers

stimulant. Also there were lots of hart's tongue ferns and wild garlic growing there, too. A solitary heron was engrossed in looking for its dinner on the water's edge, then – seeing me – took off in a lumbering clumsy flight. I was very near to it – the nearest I have ever been to one, and it appeared much bigger than I imagined.

Heron alights

I came out of the forest, near the village of Ramsden which in the beginning, of course, began with a small clearing in the forest. It lies in a valley near the River Evenlode. What is now the village street – so the historians say – was once merely a cattle track and a way up to the forest and beyond. But gradually the forest was pushed back, some of the land reclaimed and little wattle cottages were built, and the inhabitants scratched out a living there: now, of course, it is a very lively thriving village. It wasn't until 1843 that Ramsden got their own church. Before this the villagers of Ramsden and neighbouring Leafield had to walk to Shipton-under-Wychwood for baptisms, marriages and burial – and this was a good six miles across the forest. And there's a story that a corpse, which was being carried and taken from Leafield village to Shipton for burial was lost for several days – the trouble was that there was this violent snowstorm, and the men set the coffin down, some say to chase rabbits, some to poach pheasants, for food was hard to come by; others say it was while they banged their hands across their chest to warm them – an expression called 'baffum jack', others say to chase squirrels. Anyhow, when the men went back to

Hart's tongue fern

Two different species of orchid

resume their task, the coffin couldn't be found, and was indeed not found for three weeks. It was lost in a snowdrift!

The folk of nearby Ramsden also claim a story of the lost corpse as theirs, but wherever it happened it is quite an eerie tale.

Of course, many years ago a lot of poaching went on in and around the villages that skirt the forest. Men were often forced to do this because wages were so low and their families almost at starvation point. Fines for poaching were very heavy and the culprits were sent off to prison. Arthur Young, an agricultural economist, wrote in 1809 that, 'The vicinity around Wychwood is filled with poachers, deer stealers, thieves and pilferers of ever kind and Oxford Jail would be uninhabited were it not for this fertile crime.'

But not all the poachers were caught. And most of the cottages were built with a huge iron bar high up inside the chimney. It was on these bars that carcasses of deer and pheasants were hung, well out of the way of the foresters who came looking for such things. And when a villager was lucky enough to get away with deer and the like, feastings with friends and neighbours followed.

Today some of the old cottages still have those huge iron bars way up in the chimney breasts, a grim reminder of those hard-up days.

Poacher

61

uly in Wychwood was almost as glorious as June was. The only difference was the fact that because we had almost three weeks of exceptionally very hot days, some of the flowers had gone over. But the trees and bushes were still green and lush. There were, however, quite a few different flowers in bloom: red hemp-nettle, enchanter's nightshade, and a tall flower called weld – or dyers rocket. It had pale-yellow flowers, but it was the dark and shiny leaves that were mostly used to

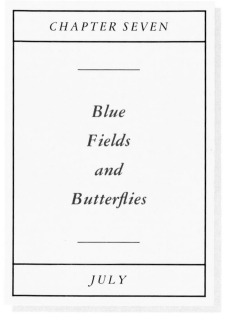

CHAPTER SEVEN

Blue
Fields
and
Butterflies

J U L Y

dye wool – hence the name dyers rocket. And on a piece of clear ground in the forest, which incidentally is called The Rutting Plain, there were masses and masses of brilliant rich gold flowers growing, known as Oxford ragwort. I wondered if the reason for the wonderful display of them this year was the fact that originally it had come from the lavas of Etna and Vesuvius, and that we have been experiencing weather as hot as is usual in their country of origin. The plants were brought to England and planted in The Physic Garden in Oxford in the seventeenth century, by a botanist. From there the seed ecaped to old walls and railway verges, now it can be found almost everywhere in the British Isles; in Scotland it is known as

Oxford ragwort on Rutting Plain

stinking willie on account of the nasty smell. At one time, volunteers were asked every year to meet on Port Meadow at Wolvercote, Oxford, to pull acres of it up as it is poisonous, and the huge meadow – just outside Oxford – is a place for free-grazing for cattle.

There is such a wonderful variety of flowers in Wychwood, some that I have never seen before. Mr Sheasby and his late wife made a recorded survey of 432 species of flora growing there. I just noticed a few in this beautiful forest.

In several places around the edge of the forest there are a number of farms. These were mostly created when the forest was enclosed in the nineteenth century. Sometimes my walks take me very near to the farm land. And today, a couple of fields caught my eye – well, I could hardly miss them! Acre upon acre of the loveliest blue – quite an unusual sight in Oxfordshire – but then farmers are now trying out different things to grow. I thought at first that it was flax, but no, it was linseed, grown, of course, for the oil value. Nearby was a field full of golden wheat whispering in the brilliant sunshine.

On Evendon pond, one of the quite small lakes, a pair of little grebe or dabchicks

Little grebe or dabchick

as they are often called, were swimming with two tiny chicks, but they soon disappeared under the overhanging foliage of the pond.

And lots of damselflies with their irridescent bluey-green wings flew around the water's edge; some larger ones which were most likely dragonflies darted about after insects, some I believe are called the devil's darning needles, because of this. I discovered that dragonflies are one of the fastest and oldest insects in the world. They can reach a speed varying from 35 to 60 mph, and remains in fossils show that they existed 300 million years ago.

I sat in the shade for a while, the temperature was in the eighties, and I was glad of a rest. High up in one of the trees I could hear a nuthatch – well, there was most likely a pair. Then, suddenly, one came head first down the tree trunk, found either a nut or an acorn in the grass and then squittered partway up the tree again. The bird placed the nut firmly into a small fork on one of the branches and sort of hammered it in with its beak, then it proceeded to peck at the shell vigorously; this he discarded and just ate the kernel. The bird made to come head first down the trunk again. At this point I thought I'd better make a move, but until that moment the little slate-grey bird with a distinct orange breast did not know that I was there.

Wandering along by one of the lakes, I noticed a number of wild honey-bees around the base of an old rotten oak tree. I stopped and took a closer look. There were dozens and dozens of them flying in and out of their nest, some with little sacs of pollen on their bodies. For a moment I wished that I was a great brown bear so that I could steal some of the honey, but on second thoughts realized that they were storing up food to eat during the winter-time.

Damselflies

Down by a stream leading into Kennel pond, I came across two more species of orchid, the pyramid and the small southern marsh orchid. There are a few other types that grow in the forest, so I hope to find more as I go along.

I wandered down by the old quarries where, at one time, tons and tons of stone were dug for building purposes. The present Cornbury Mansion, which is situated in part of the Wychwood forest, was built mostly from stone quarried here, some was also used to help build Blenheim Palace at Woodstock, and the Guildhall in London. Now the quite high quarry sides are largely covered with trees and bushes, but some of the huge blocks of stone are still visible. Today, in the brilliant sunshine, butterflies were out in their dozens. I saw lots of gatekeepers, or hedge browns as they are sometimes called; marbled white and small common blue – quite a number of them were feeding on the masses of blackberry blossom, a promise of much fruit to come in September.

And down by the old Cyder Well, at least four cock pheasants and three females were feeding and drinking in the clear spring water, so intent were they that they took no notice of me at all as I passed very near to them. (On my visits to the forest I always cup my

Honey Bee

A pair of nuthatches with acorn

Kennel pond in high summer

hands and take a drink from that particular spring, as it comes straight out of the hillside – absolute nectar!)

Suddenly along the wide green ride came the biggest flock of sheep that I've ever seen. One man on a small motorized vehicle, and three lovely sheep dogs were in charge of the huge flock. 'How many?' I called to the shepherd. 'Seven hundred and fifty,' he said, grinning back at me. They were off to pastures new and it was time I made my way towards the edge of the forest. Then, some way away I heard a strange short screeching noise coming from high up in the trees; suddenly overhead one of the buzzards flew. They are very big birds seen close at hand. He wheeled around and then was off deep into the forest, but still making this strange noise – some sort of warning note, I would think.

I made my way up to the village of Leafield, where I had arranged to meet Peter MacGregor, who

Gold watch and chain

has lived there for most of his life. He is Leafield Parish Council Chairman and Chairman of the National Association of Local Councils, and on many other large councils including the 'Keep Britain Tidy' one. He has always been very interested in village life, and regrets the passing of the old characters. He knew quite a number of them at one time and always stopped to chat to them, so he has a fund of stories about happenings in the village years ago and the happy, simple, contented way of life as it was — along with some of the dark deeds that happened in the forest!

Southern marsh orchid

'Of course,' Peter said, 'some of the tales that have been handed down may have got a bit distorted over the years. But Leafield being a bit remote from other places, was a bit of a wild place during the last century, they were truly forest folk, you see, and inter-marrying took place so that most everybody was related to somebody in the village.'

'I'll tell you one tale,' he went on, 'that folk reckoned was gospel truth. It's about a man whose parents from round here had emigrated to Australia years and years before, and he apparently had really done well for himself. So, he comes back to England to see if he could find out where his parents were born, and arrived at Charlbury station, and called at one of the inns for some refreshment before walking through the forest to Leafield. It was noted by some men in the pub that the man had a lot of money on him, and gold rings on his fingers and a wonderful gold watch and chain across his chest, but nobody knew who he was — he most likely had been born in Australia. Anyhow, the man never arrived

Marbled white butterfly

Gatekeeper or hedge brown, and common blue butterflies

in the village. A couple of days later a forester came across the very badly injured man. He was carried on a stretcher made from wood cut from a nearby tree, and they took him to The Potters Arms, a pub in Leafield.'

(The pub is still there, Peter told me, but it is now called The Spindleberry Inn.)

'Well, the poor fellow died, and nobody claimed him. He was buried in Leafield churchyard and registered in the deaths as "name not known". Years later, when I suppose they thought that the coast was clear, some of the village folk came out with the rings and jewels and a lovely gold watch and money in their pockets. Authorities were informed and the guilty party arrested – and they had to pay for their dreadful deed.'

Peter also told me some of the old characters and some nick-names used in the Wychwood villages years ago:

Sheep

Shackuts

Basket

Snobby

Corrymonger

Woodman

Stunnel

Oh Be Joyful

Doughy

Clanger

Paddle and Puddle

Bag-ass

Whistler

Jack O'lads

Bobble lads

Hurdle

Quit Quot

Squinter

Sara Jane Holy Ghost – so called because this stiff and starchy old maid was going to have a baby. When asked who the father was, she said, 'I 'ent bin with no man, I tells 'e, it must 'ave bin the 'oly Ghost.'

Fred was being visited by a rather grand local gentleman, and he, Fred, was trying to talk posh-like. So his wife said to him, 'Fer goodness sake, Fred, stop trying to crack thy bloody jaw cos he knaws who thee bist.' (Crack your jaw – put your talk on.)

Cock pheasants

An elderly couple whose cottage was situated next to the village pond, said to a young man who had done them a good turn. 'Thas very kind of you, next time you comes by the pond drop in.'

CHAPTER EIGHT

Forest

Flowers

and

Forest

Folk

AUGUST

fter a couple of heavy tropical-type storms I made my way once more to Wychwood. Along the winding country lanes that lead to the Secret Forest, blue scabious, scarlet poppies and tall pigweed or hogweed lined the verge-sides. There had been much harvesting going on in the surrounding fields, with still a lot more to be done, but not today, as everything was pretty sodden after the storms. But the next few days promised to be very hot so things would soon dry out again.

The forest looked beautiful in the bright morning sunshine; high in the heavens an exhaltation of larks were pouring out their thankfulness for the beauty of the day; a solitary noisy magpie flew overhead, so I gave him my usual nod of the head and said out loud, 'Good-morning, sir, and good-morning to your wife over the hedge', remembering that it is 'one for sorrow, but two for joy' – that way, including the wife bit, makes it joyful.

Down one of the rides there was quite a lot of tall burdock growing; its tiny red flowers were out, but later on the seed – the very sharp-hooked prickly 'burs' – will

WYCHWOOD
The Secret Cotswold Forest

Looking down to Five Ash Bottom, with poppies and hogweed

lean out and attach themselves to any-thing passing.

Near the sawmill area I was suddenly struck by a vision of delicate blue – a huge mass of very tall flowers, some quite eight feet high, that were growing in a huge clump. There were a few white ones, among the bell-like flowers. I guessed that they were of the Campanula family, but I'd never seen them like this, growing in such profu-sion and in the wild, too. But in Mr Sheasby's account of *The Flora of Wychwood*, which I have to continually refer to as many of the forest flowers are not found anywhere else, he writes that the mass of tall bell-like flowers in that par-ticular area are '*Cam-*

Burdock and hoverfly

panula lactiflora Bieb, presumably introduced with household waste'. This is quite possible because the area is fairly near Cornbury Park and Mansion, which is part of Wychwood and owned by the same family.

The majestic beech trees which can be found in several areas in the forest were simply bowed down with beech nuts. I have never seen such a crop. At the moment they are in their browny-green protec-tive masts – come September and the three-cornered nuts will be popping out of those masts to provide squirrels, jays and pheasants with plenty of food. Already the leaves on some of the trees are beginning to turn yellow – namely the chestnut, birch and hazel. This is quite six to eight weeks earlier than usual: I

Beech nuts

Skylark and feverfew

suppose the intense heat, along with the dry periods that we have been experiencing this year, has something to do with it.

But the dry weather has not made any difference to the honesty plant, for it was climbing everywhere. At the moment it is covered with sweet-smelling greenish-white flowers, which will later turn into feathery seed heads, commonly known as old man's beard. But the nicest name for

Flower of traveller's joy

the plant, I think, is traveller's joy, so called because – according to an eighteenth-century writer – of its 'decking and adorning waies and hedges where people travel'.

But this is surely the month of the thistle. I found eight different varieties of them, all blooming magnificently purple. Some had very big flower heads, like the Scottish emblem, while others were quite small – woolly-headed, spear and plumed – to name just a few. Of course, the wild flowers that grow in this beautiful forest survive because much of it is a nature reserve. But the thistles that grow in fields are a bit of a nuisance to farmers. Seeing so many of them growing in profusion reminded me of an old rhyme about thistles:

> Cut 'um in May they'll spoil yer hay,
> Cut 'um in June 'tis a bit too soon,
> Cut 'um in July, then 'um 'ull die.

Patches of lovely, pale pink mallow flower were also growing around there. When the flower goes to seed it forms a shape like a little round cheese. As children we gladly gobbled these up – goodness only knows what it did to our insides!

There were plenty of corn marigolds and feverfew growing, too – some folks reckon that the leaves of the feverfew, eaten in sandwiches, are good for easing migraine. And nearby, teasels as tall as a man were growing.

'Sitty' hen

Goldfinches feeding on thistles

They were in bloom and covered in very small, pale mauve flowers on which several bees were feeding.

On my way home, I stopped at the village of Chilson, which many years ago was part of the forest. I called to see retired Wychwood head-keeper, eighty-eight-year-old Charlie Barnes, who is bedridden, but he talked to me for a little while about the time when he worked in the forest, and when he had seven, and sometimes nine, keepers under him. This was when Mr Watney was the owner. 'Did you get many poachers in there?' I enquired.

'Poachers! oh yes, dozens of 'um during the shooting season. It got that bad that we had to take it in turns to stay up all night, hoping to catch 'um. I organized it so that three of us was on duty every third night. Used to meet up by the big old oak tree at Watermans Lodge on the Leafield road, and sit up in the trees in different places in the forest where we knew the poachers was likely to come in.'

'Did you catch many?' I asked.

'Oh, yes. We caught a fair few, hawled 'um up to Chipping Norton to the magistrates court. A fellow called Chamberlain was one of the JPs at the time – nice fellow, he was, very fair. It was he who fined the poachers and gradually we *nearly* wiped out poaching there. 'Course it was much harder work, being a keeper in them days,' he went on. 'We had to hatch out all our own pheasants, [I remember keeper Bill Archer telling me about this] nowadays the Estate owners buys a lot of their chicks in, then they brings 'um on in heated houses. But when I was keepering we had to go all round the countryside buying up broody hens [sitty or sitting hens, they are sometimes called]. Well, we sort of borrowed 'um really just for a month or two. What we did was call round the villages and ask people if they'd got a broody [sitty] hen; we paid 'um 2/6d each, and we used to sit 'um on a dozen or more pheasants eggs. The old hens would sit tight and after three weeks bring the young chicks off and then the old hens would stay in a pen and run along with the young pheasants 'til the young 'uns was old enough to be left. Then we'd take the hens back to their owners. One old gel in the village

Magpie

Game-keeper in tree out to catch poachers

always let me have two or three sitty hens every year. 'Course *I* couldn't pay 'er for 'um, I had to wait 'til the agent give it to me first. Wages wasn't that big that I could afford to pay anybody out of my money. Well, the weeks went by, and one day I was in Charlbury talking to a rather important gentleman about the shooting season, when up this old gel comes, jumps awf her bike and said in a loud voice, "Well, Mr Barnes, when be you going to pay me that money you owes me?" Well, I wished the ground had opened up and took me with it! "Sorry," I said, "I haven't been given it yet." "Well, you tell 'um to hurry up or I shan't let 'um have any more sitty hens," and she pushed her pedals round with her hands to make it easier to mount her old bike.

'A few days later the agent gave me the old gel's money, and the rest that I had to pay out to the other folk – but I 'ung on to 'ers for three or four weeks, I thought, "let the old bugger wait". Anyhow, the next year she comes sidling up to me – mind you, 'er hadn't spoken to I since I give 'er 'er dues last year, and 'er says, "Hello, Mr Barnes, I've been wanting to see you. I got four broody hens for you, sitting as tight as tight they be." "Sorry," I says to 'er, "we got all we wants this year." 'Er never offered I any more arter that.'

SNIPPETS FROM THE WYCHWOOD AREA

I am grateful to Ruth Kench of Chilson, for this extra information about Charlie Barnes (retired head-keeper in Wychwood) and for other stories that she gleaned from him.

Charlie Barnes, who is eighty-eight years old, was born in Frog Lane at Milton-under-Wychwood; before he left school he worked for a local butcher (before school in the morning and after at night), and on Saturdays – for this he earned one shilling a week. After several jobs he decided that he wanted to be a keeper and in 1925 went to work for Mr Watney (senior) who had bought Cornbury Park and Mansion and Wychwood forest in 1900.

Mr Watney died in Scotland while on a deer shoot: apparently his gillie pointed out a deer, and, as he lifted his gun to shoot, Mr Watney dropped down dead.

He left all his workers £9 each – at that time, wages were only £2 a week so the £9 must have seem quite a windfall. Mr Watney's son, O.V. Watney, inherited the estate, and Charlie stayed on and worked for him.

Charlie said that they used to shoot rabbits, cats, squirrels, foxes, magpies, jackdaws and carrion crows. And 'trap' weasels, stoats and moles. The foxes, moles and weasels had to be skinned straight away. These were nailed on his garage door and dried, so Charlie made a bit of money when he sold the skins. But this method was stopped when the law banned the killing of certain animals. In the forest the birds and vermin that were caught were hung up on a string line; to show your boss that you were doing your job properly. Charlie used ferrets and snares as well as shooting the vermin. Small brown owls who had nests in holes in the trees, were shot, as they were very destructive in killing the young pheasants to feed their young. But barn owls were left alone as they do a good job in catching rats and mice along the hedgerows.

Charlie said that during the 'game' season they had to be up all night to watch for the poachers who mostly came from Finstock and Leafield. One noted poacher was Tommy Chapman from Charlbury. The Wychwood keeper at that time employed him one day as a beater. When asked why he had *him*, he replied, 'If I didn't, he'll be watching in which direction we are, and go somewhere else, and help himself to our birds – this way I knows where he is.'

Woman on bike

A gentleman, Lord Dillan, asked Chapman – knowing him too well, 'How are *you* Chapman?' He replied, 'Fit as a rat in a sink, sir.' Tommy Chapman was a very heavy drinker often going to The White Hart in Charlbury for this. One day, there was an Italian with a barrel-organ playing outside the pub. The man had a live monkey who sat at the top of the organ. Someone bet Tommy a gallon of beer that he couldn't shoot the animal. He took a pistol from his pocket and shot at the monkey through the window of the pub and killed it. The Italian stayed about a long time and threatened to kill the man if he could catch him – but he never did.

Monkey

If you had an allotment at Finstock you were not allowed to kill anything on that land. One poor man shot a hare and someone told Dingle, the keeper, about it. The man who had 'let on' had a small stack of hay on his allotment. Next day it was all burnt down, with a message to say 'A Dore never forgets'. (Dore was, and still is, an old Finstock family name.)

One of Charlie Barnes's special stories –

Years ago the owners of Wychwood used to sell poles from the forest for making hurdles. One man, Puddle from Fifield, who was famous for his hurdle-making, went and bought some of these poles. But he left it too late, to get out of the forest while it was light, and got completely lost, and kept wandering about in the dark shouting, 'Lost! Lost!' and an old owl hooted, 'whooo, whooo'. The man answered 'Its me, Puddle from Fifield, you fool!'

King John hunted in the forest and he used to bring the horses up to Kings Standing, opposite the Ascot-under-Wychwood turn, to stable them. Charlie said that once some men were digging up there, and found a skeleton of a man who was eight feet long.

Mr O.V. Watney left Charlie Barnes his cottage to live in rent-free for his lifetime.

Ruth Kench's father was also left his cottage to live in rent-free for his lifetime by Mr Watney. Ruth's father was gardener at Rangers Lodge when Mr Fellows, the estate agent for Cornbury, lived there. Ruth still lives in the cottage but, of course, not rent-free any-

Stoat

more. Her father died some years ago, aged ninety. But Ruth has lived in the village of Chilson for the past sixty years and has seen many changes. Gone are the village school, post office, off-licence, travelling shop that sold everything – and water is no longer carried by hand from a spring at the top of the hill. Water and sewers came to the village fifteen years ago. Cottages that once held big families are now mostly weekenders. But there are still a couple of farms in the village.

Barn owl

Beech

nly two weeks had passed since my last visit to the Secret Forest, and yet quite a lot of changes had already taken place. One thing that struck me was the fact that the thistles, which last month had been all purple and royal, had, for the most of them, gone over. Now, in place of the flowers were beautiful tufts of seed heads where goldfinches and linnets were busily feeding. In this state the thistle seeds reminded me of a story that my mother told me long ago. It happened

CHAPTER NINE

Autumn
Crocus
and
Larch
Cones

SEPTEMBER

when she was young – about ten years old she was at the time. Each late summer, her mother would send her off 'wool gathering' – no! not the state that we sometimes find ourselves in, inattentive and in a dreamy mood when the mind wanders, but to gather and collect sheep's wool that had been caught on hedges, barbed wire and blackberry bushes. This, when it had been washed was used to fill cushions, pillows and even mattresses for children's beds. 'And don't come back till you've filled your bag,' her mother would say. The bag, a home-made affair, was made of hessian from an old sack that her father had brought home. This day, in particular, was hot and humid, and my mother said that she had walked miles and

Linnet on thistle seed heads

miles and not got the bag anything like full. Then she saw a field absolutely full of thistles gone to seed, and these gave her an idea. First, she tipped her gathered wool out and left it on the side of the field. Then she set about and gathered as much of the thistle seeds as she could. Then she carefully piled the sheep's wood on the top so that it looked as if she'd got a bag full. Her mother was quite pleased, 'You shall have a nice piece of seedy cake as a reward,' she cried. But, a few hours later, when her mother tipped out the wool to wash it and discovered the thistle seeds – which by then had gone flat – the mood was very different! A good hiding followed, and then it was off to bed for the rest of the day.

Ling and mint

Down one of the main rides the ground was absolutely carpeted with ling, a pink heather-like flower, and a bit further along on 'Ussels' bank, strong-smelling, purple mint was growing in abundance, and the combination of the colours of the ling and mint were quite beautiful.

And at last the meadow saffron (*Colchicum autumnale* to use its proper name) but known locally as autumn crocus – was blooming. (They are also called naked nannies or naked ladies because they have no leaves surrounding them.) Carpets and carpets of delicate pale mauve flowers, but once the deer start on them many of the flowers will disappear, as they probably find them nice and sweet.

Mr Sheasby, in his account of *The Flora of Wychwood*, calls the autumn crocus 'One of the glories of the forest', and I agree with him.

The day was warm and balmy, a lone

Picking thistle seeds

sparrowhawk hovered overhead, and young pheasants were running about in their hundreds. In one area I saw a startlingly black and white one, most likely a special species, I would think, brought in to mate with the ordinary ones.

This month I saw several deer, one group of about six had a very young one with them; it was about a couple of months old, I would think, and although I kept perfectly still, not even moving a muscle, they knew I was there – perhaps by smell. Anyhow, the majestic stag in the group suddenly held his head upright looking in my direction, then in a flash they all disappeared into the forest glade.

And whether it was something to do with the long hot summer or not, but it was literally raining fir cones – well, larch cones they were – the forest path was littered with hundreds and hundreds of them, and still they were falling on me as I walked along.

And already, on some of the early variety of elder, the berries were black and ripe, quite a couple of months earlier than usual. In other cases, the elder bushes were dying – this, I suspect, is because they are shallow rooted.

There seemed to be dozens and dozens of daddy-long-legs flying around, you

Autumn crocus or naked ladies as they are known locally

Female sparrowhawk

never seem to see them at any other time of the year, when they hatch out from eggs and pupa of the leather-jacket. They always remind me of Witney Feast – always held on the first Monday after the first Sunday after the eighth of September. It was, of course, around this date that the famous Forest Fair was held in Wychwood – from 1790 until 1855 – but some say it ended in 1857. And the reason that this Forest Fair originated – well, so the story goes – was that some religious families living in nearby Witney thought that the Witney Feast was a terrible place to take their children, it was full of ruffians and pick-pockets and naughty side-shows.

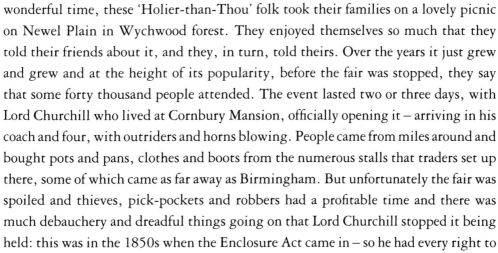

Peewits

So, while everyone else went off to the feast and had a wonderful time, these 'Holier-than-Thou' folk took their families on a lovely picnic on Newel Plain in Wychwood forest. They enjoyed themselves so much that they told their friends about it, and they, in turn, told theirs. Over the years it just grew and grew and at the height of its popularity, before the fair was stopped, they say that some forty thousand people attended. The event lasted two or three days, with Lord Churchill who lived at Cornbury Mansion, officially opening it – arriving in his coach and four, with outriders and horns blowing. People came from miles around and bought pots and pans, clothes and boots from the numerous stalls that traders set up there, some of which came as far away as Birmingham. But unfortunately the fair was spoiled and thieves, pick-pockets and robbers had a profitable time and there was much debauchery and dreadful things going on that Lord Churchill stopped it being held: this was in the 1850s when the Enclosure Act came in – so he had every right to stop it. When the last fair was held there, ten excursion trains brought people to Charlbury station.

Here are two accounts from old papers about the Forest Fairs:

Apparently each year there was an election held to choose a Fair Maid of Wychwood. In the old days, according to local legend, the Fair Maid had a pretty rough time. When chosen, she fled through the Wychwood forest pursued by local youths,

Fir cone

Fallow deer

rogues and vagabonds. Her captor, it is said, was then free 'to have his way' with her!

The Forest Fair was held in the middle of September, and in its heyday attracted an average attendance of well over twenty thousand people. The shows and booths at the fair had to be set up leaving a broad space for the passage of the long procession of coaches, headed by those of the Duke of Marlborough and Lord Churchill, which opened the week's festivities.

Daddy-long-legs

There were stalls which sold cloth unobtainable in the district at other times, several booths sold only hand-spun linen for making smocks, while cheapjacks, pedlars and chapmen of all kinds cried their wares. Special china mugs marked 'Forest Fair' were also obtainable. Another attraction of the fair was fighting. The ring was a space on the turf, and contestants would stand around this ring. There was money to be made by fighting, as a guinea could be earned by anyone who could win a fight.

The prize money was presumably donated by the Duke of Marlborough and Lord Churchill. A man would throw his hat into the ring as a challenge, and another hat thrown in was an acceptance of the challenge.

Many villages had a recognized champion, and these men attended the fair year after year for the purpose of fighting, as did Henry Townsend, a local man.

An attempt was made to stop Forest Fair about 1830, on the grounds that it brought into the area 'pickpockets, bullies, card sharpers and numbers of idle and disorderly characters', and a case is recorded of a card sharper being ducked in a pond until he was unconscious.

The coming of the railways brought even more rogues, and in 1855 Forest Fair was held for the last time.

Peter MacGregor also told me about an elderly man who lived in the village of Leafield,

Elderberries

in the 1940s, a Mr Pratley who was then in his late nineties; Mr Pratley told him about when he was taken to the fair as a child and what a marvellous event it was. Some of the gentry even had a huge boat or barge on one of the lakes, all lit up with an orchestra playing.

During the last war, to help with the war effort, Newel Plain – where this wonderful fair had been held – was for the first time ploughed up and planted with corn. The men who did this thought that maybe they might find coins there, but nothing was found. But the tilling of Newel Plain did much to harm the many rare flowers that had grown there for centuries. There are still a number of rare ones that did survive along with a very big yew tree. Gazing up into the centre of the old tree with its many lovely straight, slim branches, I could see why the bows, which centuries ago helped to defend this island of ours, were made from yew wood.

Starlings

As I came out of the forest, I noticed that already some types of birds were flocking. Great sweeps of peewits were wheeling around above some newly ploughed land. And then, because it was very late afternoon, a huge flock of starlings flew overhead, most likely making for their roosting place. There must have been thousands of them, and their flight overhead was almost as if a dark cloud had passed over the sun. Seeing this great flock reminded me of the story of an elderly man who lived on the edge of a wood where every evening great flocks of starlings came in to roost. Of course, they made a noise and a mess as they glided in. He got so fed

Man with trays

90

up with this ritual that he thought of a plan to frighten the birds away, hoping that they would find another roosting place. He got two old tin trays and hung them up on his clothes line, then cut a couple of thick sticks. His plan was to stand with the trays either side of him and when the birds started to fly over he would bang them – bang-bang – very hard, with the two sticks. Well, he saw them arriving and proceeded to hit the trays with all the force he could, and the frightened birds – all of 'em – simply shit all over him, so he looked as if he had fallen in a bucket of whitewash!

Yew

Aspen

s I entered Wychwood forest on a balmy October morning, the unmistakable smell of autumn tickled my nostrils – a dank smell of decaying leaves and rotten wood. Autumn had come early this year, with many of the trees and bushes having already lost their tinted foliage, but others were beautiful: never have I seen such a galaxy of autumn hues. The colours on the hawthorn bushes ranged from rich red wine, deep gold, pale gold and amber. Nearby were many elder bushes again

CHAPTER TEN

Spiders
Webs and
Satan's
Cherries

OCTOBER

with deep red leaves to palest pink, the pink ones looked almost like delicate mother-of-pearl. And the trees of the sycamore, horse chestnut and maple were all displaying their lovely autumn shades and were also losing some of their leaves, too, along with lots of iddy iddy onkers from the chestnut trees. Even the ferns and bracken which grow on either side of the wide rides had changed from deep green to pale yellow and deep gold. We were experiencing some lovely autumn weather – what we always termed as St Luke's Little Summer – we often get this sort of weather at this time of the year, St Lukes Day being October 20th. The many hazel bushes which seem to grow all over the forest had almost lost their leaves and the nuts were dropping off the branches, some still in their green huds and others

Hazel nuts

already slipped out of them. This reminded me of a very thin old lady who had been born at Leafield and who lived next door to us, many years ago. To demonstrate how thin she was she'd pull the waist of her skirt out, and say to my mother, 'Look, Missus, I be like a ripe woodnut, I be slipping hud.'

Beech nuts, too, were dropping off in their hundreds – these will provide many of the forest animals and birds with winter food. Elder bushes were simply black with berries, although some had already been stripped of fruit by birds seeking to quench their thirst. Sloe berries, beautiful with blue-black bloom on them, looked ripe and ready to pick. This year they seem to be very small with little juice in them. I like to wait until we've had a frost or two to soften them a bit – they seem much more juicy then, and fit to make sloe wine and gin.

Cobwebs were delicately slung across my pathway, and brushed my face as I strolled along. There seemed to be cobwebs everywhere in the grass and on the bushes. Some were shaped like miniature hammocks, others were the more common sort made by the diadem spider: like delicate filigree work, they were, and still bedecked with drops of dew all over them, shining like jewels in the pale autumn sunshine. There were also

Sloes, ripe for picking

Autumn scene on Lake Superior

what I've always known as gossamer: strands of very fine cob-webs floating upright in the almost still air.

These are the dispersal flights of the small Linyphiid spiders – look closely, and you will see a minute spider attached to each thread of gossamer. But they were not the

Burrowing spiders homes

only sort to be found in the forest. Walking along one of the smaller paths, I noticed that there were tiny holes, several of them in a line on the edge of the path: the holes were about half an inch across, and these, I found out, were the homes of the tunnel spider.

Dragonflies and damselflies, some greeny-blue and others with bright orange bodies, were flying over Lake Superior or settling on the green lily pads. There were

quite a number of tall brown reed mace growing, and purple loosestrife, and rosebay willowherb, now covered in white downy seeds, graced the lakeside; on the lake water boatmen squittered – I could not see them but the movement all over the water meant that they were there.

The belladonna, or deadly night-shade, whose purple flowers I noticed earlier in the year, had now gone to seed and the plants were now covered with purpley-black berries. 'Satan's cherries' is the country name for these deadly poisonous berries. Apparently, in the sixteenth century, Venician ladies used an extract from these to dilate the

Common darter dragonfly on rose hips

pupils of their eyes – to make them more attractive to the opposite sex. And in more recent times, the plant was grown especially, and extracts from it made into belladonna syrup which was given to horses to cure coughs and colds.

While I was gazing at some fungi – a type which I had not come across before – a tiny animal peeped out at me; it was, in fact, a common shrew. He suddenly made a high-pitched squeaky sound, perhaps to warn his mate; they usually feed on insects and vegetable matter on land, but all at once the shrew, sensing danger, took a dive into the lake and swam out of sight – but, of course, he could have found food in the water as well as on land.

On my walks in the Secret Forest, I had noticed a small, white tent erected over a narrow part of Ussel stream. It was made of fine gauze material, and I wondered why it was there. Then one day I met Mr J. Campbell, carrying a large white net. We stopped and chatted. The tent, he told me, was to trap insects, so that he could ascertain what sort were living around there, and also in what quantity. There is quite a lot of research quietly going on in the forest, all the while, on the flora and fauna, and a record kept of any changes that might take place.

There were several galls on the oak trees: these are small round brown objects

Common shrew feeding among the fungi

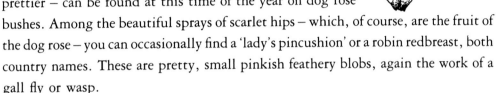

Belladonna

that we always called oak apples. They are, in fact, caused by eggs laid in the previous autumn by the gall wasp, and once used in the manufacture of ink. A similar thing – only much prettier – can be found at this time of the year on dog rose bushes. Among the beautiful sprays of scarlet hips – which, of course, are the fruit of the dog rose – you can occasionally find a 'lady's pincushion' or a robin redbreast, both country names. These are pretty, small pinkish feathery blobs, again the work of a gall fly or wasp.

October is the month when the partridge shooting starts, and of course the next month is when the pheasant shooting starts in earnest. There were many feeding and scratching about in the forest just now. Bill Archer, who was head game-keeper at nearby Swinbrook for several years, told me of an incident that happened one autumn. He said, 'I was having a wander round one day, with me gun under me arm, and I suddenly come across a complete ring of pheasants, tails down and looking very frightened. I crept up close as I could and, blow me, if there wasn't a damned great fox sat in the middle of the ring: he was waiting for one of them to move – but they seemed transfixed with fear. If one of them had moved, he'd have pounced on it and made off with it. I cocked me gun, but he must have heard the click: he took one sly look in my direction and he leaped over the frightened birds and was gone into the thickets in a flash. Never seen anything like it before, all the years I was keepering. 'Course,' he went on, 'it takes a few years afore you can become a head game-keeper. First you has to be keeper of the dogs, then keeper of the partridges, and finally of the pheasants, learning everything about all these things as you go along, and you have to know all about the woodlands and forests as well.'

He had, in the early years, started rearing his own birds, like keeper Charlie Barnes did, with a field full of

Galls on oak leaves

Partridge

hutches containing 'sitty' hens. 'Every one had to be fed and watered each morning and night – a hell of a lot more work in them days, I can tell you,' he went on, 'me missus used to help as well. Early in the mornings with the dew still on the grass, she used to get soaking wet. Still, a good drop of hot home-made wine when we got back indoors used to warm the cockles of our hearts.'

I remembered the first time I visited Bill and his wife in their old home, and we sat in their warm, welcoming kitchen. Bill's wife caught me looking at their old washing copper, that was built into the corner of the room. 'Ah,' she said, 'I'll bet you thinks that we

Rose gall or 'lady's pincushion'

still uses it to boil up the washing in, don't you?' Well, I said that it did remind me of the one that we had in the old wash-house in Ducklington, when I was young.

'Come and have a look,' she said, lifting the wooden lid off. The inside was stacked with bottles of home-made wine. 'That's our wine cooler,' she said, laughingly, 'that keeps the wine as cool as any wine cellar.'

We sampled a bottle of her autumn fruits wine, made from crab apples, sloes, elderberries and blackberries – all mixed up together. Nectar of the gods, it was!

I cycled home afterwards with no effort at all – well, in fact, I seemed to be floating along, tight as a tick I was – and thought, that if I was caught in this state I'd be charged with being drunk in charge of a bike!

Hazel

t was a typical November day when I paid my next visit to the Secret Forest, quite a nasty foggy morning with the remaining leaves from the giant beech and oak trees floating down, and from many of the other trees dropping fog was falling. But after I'd walked for about an hour, the skies began to clear and the day became quite pleasant with now and then a glimpse of pale sunshine peeping through. And down by one of the lakes the brilliant red leaves of the dogwood bushes were reflected

CHAPTER ELEVEN

Sleeping
Snails
and
Squittering
Squirrels

NOVEMBER

in the water. Also bringing colour to this November day were the dozens and dozens of sprays of scarlet hips (the fruit of the dog rose), climbing and tumbling over the bushes. During the Second World War, tons and tons of these were harvested to provide vitamin C to replace that same vitamin for children and invalids that they would have normally got from orange juice and oranges – which, of course, were almost unobtainable during the war.

Spindle-berries hung pink and lovely on the bushes; in a few weeks time the pink berries will expand to show lovely orange-coloured middles. Another thing that showed up was several different types of fungi; one species of fifty or more was in a

Autumn scene from Five Ash Bottom

group, all joined together so that they looked like a cushion – these were growing under the trees among the fallen leaves; other types – of which I must try to identify by name – seemed to spring up in front of me in a number of places.

Several grey squirrels were rummaging and squittering about under the beech trees, most likely they were collecting food for their winter store. A large flock of pigeons flew overhead and a noisy jay swooped down in front of me; they too, greedily gobble up the beech nuts.

There were not many acorns under the great oak trees and the few I did see

Spindle-berries

had sort of knobbly bits on them. Of course, years ago there were many thousands of oaks growing in Wychwood and some of the ships of the British navy were built from them. Even so, there are still a good many very fine oaks there now.

And in those far-off days some of the local farmers had common rights which allowed them to bring their herds of swine into the forest in autumn-time so that they could forage about for the acorns and beech nuts: this helped to fatten them up. And legend has it that one man, who had a goodly number of the animals, made a huge sty in the forest enclosing it with a big wattle fence, then he littered the floor with ferns and bracken to make the swine a nice comfortable bed. To get them to come back each night, he used to play tunes on his horn – he repeated this for a week or more, and then gradually the animals came back on their own,

Fungi

Grey squirrel on fir cones

without the music of the horn.

When we were young and living in Ducklington, we always kept a couple of pigs, or 'ran a couple of pigs' was the local expression; these, of course, were killed each autumn, providing our big family with plenty of fat bacon all through the winter – which was probably our salvation in those hard-up times. And always, about a month before the pigs were killed, we children were sent off down the Curbridge road to a field that we always called 'The devil's nutting ground'. In the field and in the hedges several big old oak trees grew, and we children had to pick up as many acorns as we could into the old hessian bag, affectionately called 'the devil's nutting bag'. These acorns, so our step-father said, put a good two inches of fat on the pigs – of course, the fatter the better in those days, and a twenty-score pig was quite the usual weight for a home-reared animal. And that dirty old hessian bag was hung up in the shed where the coal and wood was kept, and there it stayed getting dirtier and all cobwebby until it was needed next autumn; and an expression our mother used if we came home dirty or clapered with mud was: 'You looks as dirty as the devil's nutting bag'.

I was walking in an area where I often saw the huge Roman snails. Of course by now most of them will have crawled down old rabbit holes and sealed their shells with an almost cement-like substance, to protect them all winter long. I found one, however, that had not gone down a rabbit hole, but had sealed itself up. So I carefully covered it up with a pile of dried leaves, twigs and bracken, so that, should we get a bad winter, with luck it will survive.

When I was doing some research at Woodstock Museum on 'Folklore and medicines from the Wychwood forest', I came across this cure for a bad cough.

'A preparation of snails in salt water with cream [must have been a farmer's wife]

Jay feeding on acorns

and sugar to make an emulsion . . . An Oxfordshire woman in the Wychwood area said that she used a very similar medicine when she had a bad cough and always found it efficacious.'

And on the same page, 'For a septic finger apply lily leaves . . . and a wonderous cure for a headache – go into the forest and kill a snake, skin it and sew the skin inside your hat. You will never again have a headache.'

I think they should have added – 'first catch your snake'!

A local cure for a sty on the eye was to squeeze some juice from a garden plant called house leek, mix this with a drop of milk and bathe the eye with it.

Another cure for a sty was to pull a piece of real silk through a gold wedding ring and gently stroke the eyelid with the silk.

English small craft at the time of the Armada

This time of the year is when the poachers get busy, and again looking at the old records at Woodstock Museum, I came across quite a number of poaching tales. And one writer said that Oxford Assizes would lose half its work but for the Wychwood forest poachers.

All sorts of stories are told of the men who were so desperate to find food for their families that they went to great lengths to do so, and when they had managed to kill a deer, then came the problem, of hiding it. One hay-rick which stood out in the fields between Ascott-under-Wychwood and Shipton-under-Wychwood, had a square 'room' cut inside it and the thatch, secured to a wattle hurdle looking like the rest of the thatch, was placed on the 'roof' so that it could be lifted and replaced easily and the rick room could hold several deer. Even the old Carrier's cart had a false bottom where many a haunch of venison travelled from the forest villages to Oxford to be sold. Sometimes the forest keepers searched the villages that skirted Wychwood and they would examine the poor folks larders for cooked venison.

A young girl was staying with her granny at Milton-under-Wychwood, when suddenly a neighbour came running into the cottage carrying a big round yellow pie-dish filled with food. 'Quick,' she cried, 'put this down your gran's cellar.' When her gran came downstairs the girl told her what had happened. 'Be quiet, child,' the granny said, 'if anybody comes you don't say a word, not a word, mind you.'

And yet another tale of hiding a pie – when a raid was taking place. The big venison pie was on the kitchen table and the keepers were coming up the garden path. Quick as a flash, the wife caught up the dish, placed it on the crook of her arm and lifted her infant child, and carefully sat her on the pie and arranged its clothing so that it covered up the damning evidence – thus, saving her husband from penal servitude.

And this is another tale I came across.

A Shipton man worked on a farm lying on the edge of the forest. When returning home on a winter evening, he observed, in the dimpsey light, a fine deer grazing within gunshot of the forest wall. On the next evening it was there again; he at once reported it to correct quarters and matters were immediately put in hand. A gun was selected, the gunner engaged, sticks fixed in the wall for the man to shoot from, and the actual necessary shot was fired; before the report had dropped a terrible braying took place, and it was discovered that the supposed deer was now a dead donkey.

It belonged to some forest gypsies and a few days

Pigs eating acorns

later a poor old girl was down in the village reporting her loss and begging for help. Her tragic tale appealed to the poaching gang, and to their credit they helped her generously towards the replacement of a steed.

The stories told by the old poachers are still remembered, notably the exploit of one who claimed to be the only man who had ever been in a net with two deer. The story goes that he was hiding by the net while the deer were driven down the ride, the net being hung between two trees. A deer was driven into the net and he immediately rushed in to cut the deer's throat; before he could do so a second deer rushed into the net and the deer and man were all entangled in the net together. He managed, however, to secure both deer and, as it was impossible for him, with his companion, to carry home both deer, they hid one in the ferns while they carried the other one home, and the next night safely carried home the second deer.

From the same *Tales from the Wychwoods*, in the archives of Woodstock Museum, I found these stories that I thought worth a mention.

Ned and Nance were an old couple who lived in Milton-under-Wychwood. Nance died – apparently suddenly – so an inquest was arranged. Ned was the only witness and was asked many questions about 'the deceased'. He hadn't an idea *who* the 'deceased' was, and merely shook his head and, as the questions persisted, he ceased even to do that!

At last a more 'understanding' person said, 'Ned, tell us just what happened.' Ned woke up and said:

'Well, 'er wern't verry well, 'adn't bin for a day or two, and 'er said as 'er couldn't get up in the marnin, so I ses "Stop wur thee bist and I'll bring e summut to yet." So I made 'er a drop of brayth out o' a bit o' baäcon as we'd got and I took it up. 'Er was led vurry quiet and I ses, "Nänce," and 'er never muvved, and I ses, "Nänce, thee bistn't dyud bist?" and dalled if 'er wusn't as dyud as a nit!'

A clergyman who lived at Leafield, not long ago, told the following. One morning he was visiting an old man, and this conversation took place:

'That's a beautiful Bible, John.'

'Yessir, I uses en every daäy.'

'Well done! Will you read to me, John?'

Hay-rick

'Rade, Sir? I cyant rade!'

'But you said you use your Bible every day.'

'So I do, sir: I strops me rayzor on im.'

The same Vicar, on visiting a woman during Holy Week, discovered that she was entirely ignor-ant of the facts of the Crucifixion. He gave her such

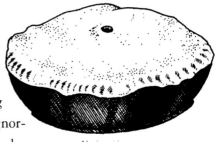
Venison pie

a graphic description of the story of Good Friday, that she was overcome with pity; then she said:

'You ses, sir, as all this 'ere 'appened long ago?'

'Oh yes, nearly 2,000 years ago.'

'Well then, sir, let's 'ope as tent true.'

Visitors to Ascott-under-Wychwood may be interested in a tree which is planted on the green, which has a seat around it. The tree was planted in memory of several women – wives of some of the farm-workers who were on strike because of low wages. This was in 1831 when wages were, in fact, only eight or ten shillings a week. Joseph Arch was the man who at that time was trying to get the farm-workers more money and urged them to go on strike until they got better pay. And it was their wives who stopped anyone else, like non-strikers, from trying to do work on the farmer's land. So the farmer, Robert Hambridge, took out a summons against the ringleaders, for obstruction and causing a breach of the peace. The women were brought before the magistrates at Chipping Norton, and, instead of just binding them over, they sent sixteen of them to Oxford Prison (making them walk all the way) and sentenced them to hard labour. There was a great cry of indignation when the news got out. The matter was even brought up in the House of Commons – after which the women were freed. But the villagers never forgot the firm stand made by them.

There was even greater sadness in the nearby village of Shipton-

Fallow deer

under-Wychwood. In 1874, seventeen people – men, women and children – set off for New Zealand for a hope of a better life for their families. They left Shipton one morning in a horse-drawn yellow farm wagon, which was to take them to the port, carrying their few belongings in makeshift bags. But the ship that they sailed in – *The Cospatrick* – sank, and all on board were drowned. There is a stone fountain on the green at Shipton in memory of those who perished. And in 1974, a beech tree was planted there to commemorate a hundred years since the sinking of *The Cospatrick* – and the loss of all those precious lives.

Oak

Spindle

 ychwood had taken on a real wintry look on what was to be my very last visit to the Secret Forest.

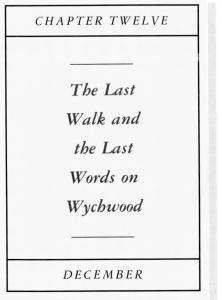

I had started out much earlier than usual because there had been a hoar frost overnight, and I wanted to see this vast woodland, all white and wonderful, before the pale winter sunshine melted it all away. And I was not disappointed, it really looked like a fairyland almost untouched except for a few marks where early birds had been walking. The air was cold, clear and freezy, and the grass all bent and straggly with the quite sharp frost.

The great beech trees looked stark and beautiful, but the bareness of almost all the trees had its compensations. Whereas in summer and early autumn the leaf cover was so dense that it was hard to see through them, now the lichen on the bare branches, and the deer were very much in evidence.

The brilliant orangey-red berries of the lords and ladies – or to use their other name – cuckoo pint, were showing up bright and lovely under the forest wall. Some of the berries were still on the bushes, the hawthorn fruits were as yet untouched by the birds and scarlet hips still climbed and tumbled in great profusion. Of course

A frosty winter scene in Wychwood

this is the time when the conifers come into their own and the red berries on the very dark green yew trees glowed like miniature lamps in the frosty air. Shiny-leafed holly bushes were berried and beautiful, contrasting sharply with the grey-looking old man's beard; dark, shiny ivy trailed over some of the dead tree trunks. However, I didn't find any mistletoe – but I am sure there was some in the vast forest somewhere.

But a mistle thrush who, among other things, feeds on the mistletoe berries, was sitting fat and beautiful on a gate post. He is the largest of the thrush family and will find plenty to eat this coming winter in Wychwood. The pheasants were not so numerous as they were last month, they have – most likely – been thinned out a bit by the big 'shoots' that take place at this time of the year.

And outside a couple of shops in nearby Woodstock were hung rows and rows of pheasants. I find them a delightful change at Christmas time instead of the usual traditional turkey.

Woodstock forest – according to Doomsday record – along with Cornbury and Wychwood, was a royal demesne forest (much later, Woodstock became Blenheim Park), and was one of the first forests to be surrounded by a wall, which was seven miles long. It was built in the twelfth

Yew berries (poisonous)

Lords and ladies showing up bright among the bare bushes

———

century by Order of King Henry I, and re-built by the Duke of Marlborough in 1727 to keep the deer in. Woodstock and the villages surrounding Wychwood have, since the sixteenth century, been famous for their glove making (which still goes on). This industry first came about because of the availability of deer skins, and Queen Elizabeth I was presented with a beautiful pair of embroidered gloves by the people of Woodstock: these are now in the Ashmolean Museum, Oxford. And our present Queen Elizabeth II was, a few years ago, presented with several pairs of hand-stitched gloves. No one knows exactly who actually had the honour of making them.

A while ago I had the privilege of meeting the manager of the last remaining glove factory in Woodstock, and he told me that six different, very skilled ladies, all 'out-workers' – which mean that they worked at home as many local women used to do – were chosen. Each were given six pairs of identical gloves to make, all in lovely pastel shades and, of course, they were all hand-stitched. And the final six pairs that were presented to Her Majesty were chosen from these.

In 1851, some gloves from Woodstock were sent to the Great Exhibition in London. They were hand-stitched by a Mrs William Boddington of Finstock and each pair of gloves would have had around two thousand stitches in them.

The holly and the ivy

Strange stories from the Wychwood area of long ago have come to light. While I was researching for this book, this story about 'Going to the Hanging' I thought was worth a mention, although I cannot trace the author of either of these two instances.

'This is a story of the days when the "hanging" was carried out in public, at Oxford; the incident was not unusual, but this occasion was marked by a disastrous conclusion. Arrangements having been made with Walker, the party were carefully instructed not to be late for the start, as on a previous occasion they had been late at Oxford and had not had a good view.

Mistle thrush and mistletoe

'A good start was made at about 12 o'clock at night in Walker Carrier's cart [the same cart which was fitted with a false bottom for the conveyance of poached venison]. The company consisted of about twelve passengers, some men and some women, who were packed in the covered cart. A halt was made at Eynsham for refreshment and to rest the horse.

'Oxford was reached early and the party had good places in the front of the crowd, from where they had an excellent view of the whole proceeding. They they separated, agreeing to meet at five o'clock for the return journey.

'Five o'clock came and several were missing, and not till much later were they all collected and packed into the cart, several of them far from sober, Walker himself very much upset and in a similar condition.

'The journey home was a very unquiet one, some were very noisy, some very sleepy and a good deal of quarrelling took place on the journey as well as the consumption of a good deal more liquor.

'Milton-under-Wychwood was at last reached and the cart came to a stop in Walker's yard [now part of the Heath Farm yard]. Walker angrily demanded that his passengers should get out. This caused great resentment, and they refused to be hurried. Walker said if they weren't soon out he would d. . .d well put them out,

Foraging pheasants

and as they didn't respond he undid the harness and the hame strap and threw up the shafts, and the whole cart-load of passengers was shot into the yard.

'The result was several broken limbs, and other injuries for which damages had to be paid by Walker. It was said that it was a long time before he made up another load for an Oxford hanging.'

And another story from Milton-under-Wychwood tells of how very desperate men were to find food during the Hungry Forties.

'Milton Quarry, where a considerable number of active labourers were employed, was notorious for its poachers; but oddly enough when the keepers wanted help it was to Milton Quarry they came for assistance. In the Hungry Forties, men wandered in large bodies through the country and frequently raided game reserves. On one occasion, Lord Dynevor's keepers came with an urgent call for help to Milton Quarry; a large number of men were known to be coming from the Black Country, and had defied all attempts to stop them, a considerable number of men joined the keepers led by a well-known "poacher" named Jack Smith: various weapons were taken, Smith taking his thrashing flail. The fight which ensued unfortunately ended in a fatality, caused by Smith hitting a man on the head with the flail.

'In court, Smith produced his billy-cock hat, of which the crown was shorn clean off by a blow from the poacher's stick, and a verdict of justifiable homicide was founded in Smith's favour and he was discharged.'

Another tale that came to light was this one from Shipton-under-Wychwood.

In 1903, Percy Manning wrote:

'At Shipton-under-Wychwood church there was many many years ago a kind of bone-house or hole where bones that were dug up in the church-yard have been put from time out of

Old stocks at Woodstock

Elizabeth I's gloves

mind. In the village many years back there was a man that others thought to be daft or not so sharp as he should be. He was challenged one night at the public house, that he dared not go to the bone-house at twelve o'clock at night and bring away a skull. The challenge was accepted and so on the given night he started. Two of the men were to go and see that he did the job. And they then hid themselves in the bone-house. At the stroke of twelve he entered and took up a head, when a horrible voice said, "Put that down, that's mine." He did put it down, and took up another, when the same voice said again, "Put that down, that's mine." "What!" he replied, "did you have two heads? then I'll have one of them," and he won his wager.'

And after that look into the past, it is time to get back to the present.

The day, after the frosty start, had turned out very pleasant and now it was time I left for home. I had been walking in the forest for several hours, but there was a sadness in my heart for this was to be my very last walk in Wychwood.

I have felt very privileged to have been able to visit the Secret Forest twice a month during 1990 to enable me to write this book, and to have learned of its ancient origins and the richness of its flora and fauna which has, thankfully, led to much of it being designated as a National Nature Reserve. This is a good thing in this age when much land and woodland is being used up in many different ways, destroying what really is our very heritage. I do hope that the present and future owners of this very special place will keep it as it is, as owners have done before them,

Carrier's horse and cart

---

by planting new trees from time to time, and at the same time preserving the wildlife and the wonderful variety of flowers, trees, fungi, lichen, animals and insects; so that maybe in, say, fifty or a hundred years time, someone else will be walking along these wide green rides where I have walked, and will be writing much as I have written about in this very special Secret Cotswold Forest.

Hawthorn

Holly

Winter in Wychwood

Winter has come
And the wild wind blows
Black are the branches
And there's snow on the wolds.

Brown is the bracken
And bare are the trees,
Crisp is the grass
Where the hoar frost gleams.

A foraging pheasant
Struts down the ride
In the pale winter sun
As the old year dies.

by Mollie Harris